THE
E S S E N T I A L
Rabbit

Consulting Editor
BETSY SIKORA SIINO

Featuring Photographs by
RENÉE STOCKDALE

HOWELL
BOOK
HOUSE

Howell Book House

A Simon & Schuster Macmillan Company

1633 Broadway

New York, NY 10019

Macmillan Publishing books may be purchased for business or sales promotional use. For information please write: Special Markets Department, Macmillan Publishing USA, 1633 Broadway, New York, NY 10019.

The Essential Rabbit is an abridged edition of *The Rabbit: An Owner's Guide to a Happy Healthy Pet,* first published in 1996.

Library of Congress Cataloging-in-Publication Data

The essential rabbit/featuring photographs by Renée Stockdale.

    p. cm.

Includes bibliographical references and index.

1. Rabbits   I. Stockdale, Renée.   II. Howell Book House.

SF453.E77   1998   98-3436

636.932'2—dc21   CIP

ISBN 0-87605-332-0

Manufactured in the United States of America

10 9 8 7 6 5 4 3 2 1

Series Directors: Dominique DeVito, Donald Stevens

Series Editors: Jennifer Liberts, Amanda Pisani

Editorial Assistant: Michele Matrisciani

Photography Editor: Sarah Storey

Production Team: Jenaffer Brandt, David Faust, Stephanie Mohler

Book Design: Paul Costello

Cover Photography: Renée Stockdale

CHAPTER ONE

What About a Bunny?

A rabbit is a fairly easy pet to own. Rabbits don't need to go on long walks every day or to be taken to obedience school. The owner of a rabbit can leave his or her pet alone for several hours a day without having to worry about the need for bathroom breaks. On the other hand, rabbits are not maintenance-free pets by any stretch of the imagination. They are social creatures that need a lot of love, attention and quality care.

THE RIGHT PET FOR YOU?

To determine whether or not a rabbit would be a good pet for you, think about your lifestyle. Will your job, school or other commitments allow you to set aside time every day to spend with your rabbit? Rabbits need daily interaction with other rabbits or with their owners to stay emotionally healthy. If you must leave a rabbit alone for many hours each day, you should probably have two rabbits, so that they can keep each other company. Are you willing to make the commitment to spend several hours a day with your rabbit or to take on the responsibility of owning two of these creatures?

RABBIT RESPONSIBILITIES

- Rabbits need daily exercise. If your rabbit will be confined to a cage or hutch most of the time, will you be able to turn her out each day for supervised activity?

- You'll need to scrub the cage every week or so, and you will have to clean out the soiled areas every day. In addition, you'll have to feed your pet and make sure

she has fresh, clean water. Can you work these tasks into your schedule?

- Think about where you live. Do you have room to house a rabbit, either outside or inside your home? Is your neighborhood zoned for rabbits? Find out before you bring home a new pet.

- If you have children, are they old enough to learn how to handle the rabbit properly and treat her with respect?

- Do you have a dog or a cat? Before you add a rabbit to your household, you should think about how your other pets will react to the rabbit, and how this new addition to your family is going to affect them.

- If you intend to have your rabbit live in the house with you, you must be willing to make changes in your environment. Rabbits are chewers, and homes that have rabbits must be rabbit-proofed.

- Consider the costs of owning a rabbit. The price of the rabbit and her cage is just the beginning. After you bring your pet home, you will have to pay for food, spaying or neutering and

The arrival of a rabbit at your home is a big responsibility; be sure you're prepared before the big day.

unlimited veterinary bills should your rabbit become ill.

- But most important of all, are you willing to make an emotional commitment to your rabbit? Are you prepared to accept responsibility for a living creature that is solely dependent on you for her well-being? Are you willing to make your pet's health and happiness a priority in your life? If your answer to these questions is yes, then you're ready to join the ranks of rabbit owners everywhere.

THE JOYS OF RABBIT OWNERSHIP

Gaining Trust

In the world of pet ownership, there are few things more rewarding than knowing that a rabbit loves and trusts you. Your rabbit's love has to be earned, though, not bought. You can only establish this kind of rapport with your pet once you have spent time with her, showing her that you are worthy of her confidence. Gaining the trust of a rabbit can be difficult; rabbits are prey animals, and are therefore suspicious by nature. How else would they survive in the wild? They are often fearful

and nervous, but once assured of their safety, the depths of their personalities come shining through.

Rabbit Intelligence

Intelligence is a quality often attributed to rabbits in popular legends, and rightly so. These bright creatures have complex social structures and develop relationships with individual people and even animals of other species. This high level of intelligence dictates that those living with rabbits must not become complacent toward their pets. Rabbits are active, inquisitive and always exploring their environment. They are notorious for opening doors, uncovering boxes and climbing into open drawers. Although endearing, this kind of behavior can get a rabbit into trouble. This is why you, as a rabbit owner, need to be especially vigilant about keeping track of your pet's whereabouts at all times.

Rabbits Can Be Trained

Many people find it surprising to discover that rabbits can be taught their names. Rabbits can also learn to understand other words and can be trained to do a variety of tricks.

3

Using a litter box and other behaviors can also be part of a well-trained rabbit's repertoire.

FINDING A RABBIT

When it's time to embark on your journey to rabbit ownership, you have several options from which to choose your new pet.

Adoption

If you are simply looking for a pet rabbit rather than a purebred show prospect, you should first consider adoption. Just as with dogs and cats, there are homeless rabbits that need loving families. They deserve a second chance with a family who will love and care for them.

If you would like to adopt a rabbit, call the animal shelters in your area and inquire as to whether any rabbits are available for adoption. Because unwanted rabbits are euthanized at shelters just like dogs and cats, adopting a rabbit directly from a shelter means you will be saving a life.

You may also want to check the "pets" section of your local newspaper, as well as bulletin boards in local supermarkets, veterinarians'

offices and pet-supply stores to see if there are rabbits in need of homes. Through a private individual, you may find a rabbit that is already litter-box trained and spayed or neutered.

A group called the House Rabbit Society was formed in the 1980s to address the problem of unwanted rabbits and now works to rescue rabbits that are about to be destroyed in animal shelters. If you want to provide a rabbit with an indoor home and have been unable to find an adoptable rabbit in an animal shelter or through a private individual, the House Rabbit Society can refer you to a local chapter of its organization, which will then put you in touch with someone who has rabbits in need of new homes. (See chapter 12 for information on how to contact this organization.)

Breeders

If you have seriously considered rabbit ownership and would like to show your pet, purchasing is also an option. The best place to buy a rabbit is from a responsible breeder—a rabbit fancier who has researched bloodlines before breeding his or her rabbits, and who keeps his or her animals in a clean and healthy living environment. These breeders are experts on their breed of choice, and frequently show their animals. Once you have determined which breed you want, you can obtain the name and phone number of a breeder in your area by contacting the national club for each breed. (See chapter 12 for more information regarding these clubs.)

Your local 4-H group is another possible source for breeders. Call your local county extension office (listed in your telephone book) and ask for the name and number of a 4-H rabbit leader in your area. This person should be able to put you in touch with a breeder nearby.

Buying from a breeder offers an added bonus: Once you purchase your rabbit, you go home with the name and phone number of an experienced rabbit owner who can answer your questions and help you with your rabbit should you have any problems.

Age

Age is another factor to consider when buying a rabbit. Although baby rabbits are adorable, they are

also more fragile and harder to train than adults. Adolescent rabbits (under 1 year) are known for being mischievous and sometimes difficult to handle. Adult rabbits, on the other hand, can make wonderful pets. Because the average rabbit's life span is from 6 to 10 years, you can adopt or purchase a rabbit that is several years old and still have a lot of time left to spend with your new friend.

If your heart is set on getting a baby rabbit, make sure the one you buy is at least 8 weeks old. Taking young rabbits away from their

Rabbits are a popular Easter gift, but they deserve more than just a short-lived holiday commitment from their owners.

5

mothers before the babies are 2 months of age can be both emotionally and physically damaging to the young rabbit. Prematurely removed rabbits rarely survive for long once they arrive in their new home.

Assessing Your Rabbit's Health

It's important to start out by selecting a rabbit that is in good health. A rabbit's general health can be determined in a number of ways. Check to see if her ears and nose are clean and free of discharge and debris. Then, take a close look at her fur.

The fur of a healthy rabbit will be soft, shiny and even. Keep an eye out for ear and skin mites, bald spots and signs of diarrhea under the tail and in the rabbit's cage or litter box.

Feel the rabbit's body. Beware of the rabbit that feels too thin, rather than round, tight and smooth. Check to see if her abdomen is hard and distended. A potbellied rabbit may be suffering from a worm infestation.

The rabbit's mental state is also an important factor to observe when determining her health. Look for an animal that is bright-eyed, alert and active. A rabbit that appears dull and listless is likely to be ill.

Look at the rabbit's teeth and determine whether the two top teeth overlap the two lower teeth. Misaligned teeth do not wear down properly, and require repeated professional treatment.

Be sure to take notice of the rabbit's surroundings. Are they clean and relatively odor-free? Are the animals kept in spacious, airy cages? Do the other rabbits appear healthy? Many rabbit diseases are contagious. If the rabbit you are considering for purchase is housed near a sick rabbit, chances are good that your

A healthy rabbit will have a bright-eyed expression and soft, shiny fur.

rabbit will come down with the same illness.

Personality

If you give your rabbit love and attention, she will most likely become a wonderful pet. However, when you are selecting your rabbit, you may want to observe the personality of the animals you are considering to see which one strikes your fancy. Rabbits that appear nervous and afraid may be high-strung, or simply unaccustomed to being handled. If the animal is young, she is still very impressionable and will learn to be held and stroked if you show her love and consideration. Older rabbits that have not been handled much will require more time, effort and patience from their owners before they feel comfortable with people. Eventually, however, they can become accustomed to being touched and should learn to respond to care and affection.

Male or Female

There is much debate in rabbit circles over which make better pets:

males or females. The answer really depends on what you plan to do with your rabbit.

Does (females) are said to be territorial and aloof. Their main concern in life is reproducing. Breeding is so important to them that some females, when not bred, will actually experience false pregnancies. Bucks (males), on the other hand, are thought to be aggressive and unsettled. Much like male cats, they have the unpleasant tendency of marking their territory by spraying odorous urine.

You can solve these problems in your rabbit of either sex quite simply: Have your rabbit spayed or neutered. Once this is done, those troublesome behaviors will disappear, the rabbit will be healthier and you will have a more gentle, loving pet. Preventing your pet from having a litter of kits will help curb the rabbit overpopulation problem and reduce the number of rabbits put to sleep in animal shelters. Spaying and neutering will also eliminate the need to choose between getting a male or female pet; spayed females and neutered males make equally good pets.

CHAPTER TWO

Homecoming

You've chosen the rabbit that you are going to adopt or purchase. Before you bring him home, you will need to prepare his environment. Shopping for and setting up all the equipment and supplies you'll need for your rabbit in advance of his arrival will make his introduction to your home less stressful for both of you.

THE CAGE

The first and most important item to purchase is your rabbit's hutch or cage. If you are buying an outdoor hutch, this will be your most significant financial investment. Take your time finding the one that best suits your needs. You can also consider building it yourself. If you decide on this option, leave yourself plenty of time to construct it before its inhabitant arrives. You should also purchase or create a nestbox for your rabbit. This will help him feel more secure.

A number of accessories are required for your rabbit's care.

CAGE AMENITIES

Your rabbit will need more than just a cage to live a comfortable and healthy life. There are a number of cage accessories that you should purchase before his arrival.

Food Dishes

Your rabbit's food bowl is very important and should be chosen wisely. Don't use just any old dish you have in the cupboard, as rabbits will chew up or knock over the wrong kind of food container. Instead, take a trip to your local pet-supply store and buy a ceramic crock made specifically for pets. Ceramic crocks are difficult to knock over and are chew-resistant.

The size of the crock you should buy will depend on the size of your rabbit. Don't buy a dish that's too small for a large rabbit to put his head into, or one that's too big for a small rabbit to reach into comfortably.

Another option for a food dish is a metal bowl that attaches to the side of the cage. Make sure that the bowl you select is shallow enough to allow the rabbit to reach all the way into it. Attach the bowl low on the side of the cage so that the rabbit is able to eat from it easily.

HOUSING TIPS

- Clean your rabbit's cage or hutch regularly.

- If you provide a blanket for your rabbit's bedding, check to make sure he's not chewing on it.

- If your hutch is wooden, make sure the interior is covered with wire to prevent your rabbit from gnawing on the wood.

- Don't place the cage or hutch in an area of excessive heat or cold.

- Keep the hutch or cage away from drafts.

- Make sure the cage or hutch is free of sharp edges and corners.

- Rabbit-proof the interior of your home if you plan to have your rabbit indoors; remove exposed wires, cords and dangerous chemicals.

- Make sure the cage or hutch is large enough to house the rabbit's necessities while providing sufficient space for the rabbit to move around freely.

- Don't place the cage or hutch in an area of continuous or excessive activity or noise.

Water Bottles

Another necessity for your rabbit's cage is a water bottle. Gravity water bottles are readily available in pet-supply stores. These are the best type of water containers for rabbits because they are impossible to knock over and they keep the water clean by protecting it from food or other matter.

When you purchase a water bottle for your rabbit's cage, make sure that it is not too small. You want your rabbit to drink as much water as possible to maintain his health. The only way to ensure this is to make sure the water bottle is always full. It's easiest to have a larger bottle, especially if you are away from home for most of the day; an inadequately sized bottle will need filling more than once daily.

Also, make sure the water bottle you purchase has a metal ball inserted into the tip. This will prevent the water from leaking into your rabbit's cage.

Hay Rack

A hay rack is another important item for your rabbit's cage. Hay is a vital element in your rabbit's daily diet. A hay rack will hold the hay in place so that it doesn't get scattered throughout the cage. Hay racks are usually made of metal and are constructed to attach to the top side of the cage. The rabbit can pull strands of hay from the rack whenever he gets the urge to munch.

Bedding

You'll want to have bedding on hand for your rabbit as well. Rabbits enjoy sleeping on straw or wood shavings. Straw can be obtained from a feed store, while wood shavings made especially for small animals can be purchased in any pet-supply shop. If you use straw or wood shavings, don't be alarmed if your rabbit nibbles on his bedding. You can also use a blanket for your rabbit's bedding. Some rabbits love to lay on or under blankets. Just be sure that your rabbit doesn't chew on the blanket, because swallowing cloth fibers is dangerous to his health.

Chewing Blocks

Rabbits are gnawing mammals, and you should provide your rabbit with something safe and chewable to satisfy his munching instincts. The best things to use are chewing blocks. Untreated wood is satisfactory, but the safest items are commercially prepared wood blocks or

11

Having a baby gate on hand can be helpful for those times when you want to let your rabbit out of his cage, but need to keep him confined to a certain area of the house.

chews, available in pet-supply stores. Offered in a variety of colors and shapes, these safe and inexpensive gnawing treats are made especially for this purpose.

Toys

You needn't buy expensive toys for your rabbit; an ordinary paper bag can be just as much fun to play with.

Many people are surprised to learn that rabbits love to play with toys. A toy for a rabbit can be anything from an empty toilet paper roll to a commercially made cat toy complete with squeaker. Having a few items on hand when your rabbit arrives will help him feel at home in his new environment. Although he might not play with these items right away, once he becomes acclimated to his new environment, he will appreciate their presence.

TRAVEL CARRIER

You should purchase a travel carrier before your rabbit makes the trip home with you, as you may need to use it for that journey. Special carriers are made just for rabbits, but these are used primarily for show rabbits and are not readily available. If you can't find a rabbit carrier, opt for a traditional cat carrier instead. Make sure you line the carrier bottom with newspaper so the rabbit won't slide around during the car ride home. This carrier will also come in handy for trips to the veterinarian and for confining your rabbit whenever you clean his cage or need to keep him temporarily in a small space. A good carrier is a wise investment.

GROOMING SUPPLIES

Rabbits need regular grooming, and thus a brush or comb should be on

your shopping list. A slicker or pin brush is best for brushing rabbit fur. This type of brush is gentle yet effective at removing snarls and mats.

If your rabbit is a shorthaired breed, a flea comb (the type used for cats) will be the best tool for combing him. If your rabbit is of a longhaired variety, you'll need a wide-toothed comb rather than a fine-toothed flea comb.

Because a rabbit's toenails need to be trimmed on a regular basis, make sure to have a nail trimmer on hand. The guillotine type used for cutting cats' nails will work, although many rabbit owners prefer to use nail clippers for humans instead.

FOOD

A supply of food (not more than one month's worth) should be on hand. Find out what your rabbit has been eating in his previous home and begin by offering him these same items. If you need to change his diet, you'll have to do so gradually over a period of a few weeks so as not to upset his digestion. (See chapter 4 for information on what to feed your rabbit.)

LITTER BOX

A litter box is another necessity if you are planning to litter-box train your rabbit. A litter box made for a cat can be good for use with a rabbit, provided that the box is not too large. A giant-size breed will do fine with a standard-size kitty litter box, but a dwarf or small breed rabbit will need a smaller box.

GETTING YOUR NEWCOMER ACCLIMATED

When your new rabbit comes into your home for the first time, it will be an exciting moment. Everyone in the family will be anxious to touch his soft fur and watch him investigate his new environment.

As exhilarating as this moment will be, it is important to realize that your rabbit will have a different perspective on the situation. He's just been taken from his familiar surroundings, stuck in a box and whisked away to a new place that he's never seen. Everything is new to him. There's little doubt that he will be feeling rather overwhelmed.

13

Because of the rabbit's built-in need to always be on the alert for predators, you may notice that your new pet seems skittish and fearful in his new environment. Remember that this is normal rabbit behavior. Your pet will need a lot of love, patience and understanding to learn to relax. Be sure to give him a place to hide while he is being introduced to his new situation. This will provide him with much-needed security.

HOW TO HOLD YOUR RABBIT

- Never pick up a rabbit by his ears.
- Slide one hand under the rabbit's front paws in the direction of his hind end.
- Place your other hand on the rabbit's rump.
- Lift the rabbit up, supporting the entire body with both hands.
- Hold the rabbit against your torso with his head facing the crook of your arm.
- Tuck the rabbit under your arm like a football and slide the hand underneath his body toward his hindquarters to support him from head to tail along your forearm.
- Place your other hand on the rabbit's back to secure him.

The kindest way to let your rabbit get acquainted with his new home is to leave him alone for a while. Place him in his cage, which will be equipped with food, water and everything he'll need to survive, and then just let him check things out in privacy for a few hours. After your rabbit has had a chance to get comfortable in his new cage, you can then begin to quietly observe him. Speak to him softly every so often to reassure him that everything is okay and let him get accustomed to your voice.

Kids and Rabbits

If you have children, this is a good time to start teaching them how to treat their new rabbit. Explain to them that their new pet needs peace and quiet so he can learn to feel at ease in his new home. Be sure that your children understand that they should not handle the rabbit right away. Because the new rabbit will be fearful and skittish, any attempts to hold him may result in injury to both child and rabbit. It's vital that you first learn the proper way to handle a rabbit, teach your children to emulate your behavior and then supervise the children while they handle the rabbit. It is not recommended that very small children (under 8 years old) be permitted to pick up or carry a rabbit. Petting a rabbit while it has all four feet safely on the floor is a better activity for very young children.

If your children are anxious to show their new rabbit to their friends, ask their friends to come in to visit one or two at a time so as not to scare the animal. They should be as quiet as possible when they are near the new rabbit, because rabbits' ears are very sensitive; loud noises can frighten them.

HANDLING YOUR RABBIT

Rabbits do not like to be lifted and held unless they are gradually taught to tolerate it. If your rabbit has not been held very much in his life, it will require skill and patience to teach him to accept being held.

Because rabbits are not natural climbers, your pet will feel awkward and insecure when lifted off the ground. As a result, he will struggle frantically or kick out violently. A fall can seriously injure a rabbit and so can violent kicking, which may

result in a broken back. It is for these reasons that you must learn to hold your rabbit properly and securely. (Before you practice picking up and carrying your rabbit, be sure to wear protective clothing. Bare skin and rabbit nails don't mix!)

There are several correct ways to hold a rabbit, depending on the size of the rabbit and how comfortable the animal feels when being held. One common method is to slide one hand underneath the rabbit's chest between his front

The most important thing to remember when picking up your rabbit is to support his back legs.

paws, with your fingers facing the hind end. Place your other hand on the rabbit's rump. Lift the rabbit with your hand under his chest while supporting his hind end with your other hand. Hold the rabbit against your torso with his head facing the crook of your elbow. Tuck the rabbit under your arm as if he were a football. Then slide your hand under his chest along his underside until your hand is supporting his hindquarters. Place your other hand on the rabbit's back to secure him. This is a good carrying position that feels safe to the rabbit.

Another method that works with smaller rabbits is to take hold of the animal's scruff (the loose skin on the back of the neck) with one hand, and place your other hand under his rump. As you begin to lift the rabbit by the scruff, support the weight of his hind end with your other hand. Bring the rabbit close to your body right away to provide him with security. (This method only works well for rabbits that don't kick when they are held.)

Remember when handling your rabbit to always treat him gently and carefully.

INTRODUCING OTHER PETS

Rabbits are very sociable animals. In the wild, they live in large groups and have a complex social hierarchy. They therefore can get along very well with other pets, including cats, dogs and other rabbits. However, whether or not there is harmony in a particular multi-pet household depends largely on the individual animals involved, as well as the owner.

If your rabbit is going to live in your house and have the opportunity to move about freely, he will need to get along with your other pets. It can take considerable time, patience and commitment to teach your dog or cat to get along with a new rabbit. Never try to force this process and always supervise your animals when they are interacting together.

Dogs

When it comes to dogs, rabbit owners have to take special care. Dogs and rabbits are natural enemies; dogs are predators and rabbits are prey animals. It is instinctive for dogs to chase and even kill rabbits,

and it's instinctive for rabbits to fear dogs and run from them. If you are going to keep both a rabbit and a dog as pets, you need to be aware of this inherent tension between the two creatures.

If you already have a dog and would like to bring a rabbit into your home, you should consider your dog's personality. Dogs that are older and calmer usually adjust more easily to the introduction of a new pet. A quiet, elderly dog is less likely to chase a rabbit.

If you do have a young, easily excitable dog, rabbit ownership may still work out for you provided you are able to control your dog. During the introduction process, you will have to be able to contain your dog's enthusiasm. If she typically ignores you when you call her and basically marches to her own drummer, you will have a problem when

Introducing your new rabbit to family members and other pets can be fun, but should be done slowly.

trying to introduce a new rabbit to the home.

Assuming that your dog is controllable, think about her past relationships with other animals. Is she aggressive toward cats? Does she like to chase rabbits when you take her camping? Does she receive encouragement to do this? If your answer to these questions is yes, you will have a difficult time teaching your dog that the new rabbit is paws-off, as she has already spent considerable time learning that it's okay to chase smaller animals. You can certainly give it a try, but you may have to consider keeping the two animals apart indefinitely or simply passing on rabbit ownership.

If you have determined that your dog's temperament will allow her to make friends with a rabbit, you can begin the gradual process of introducing the two animals. Start the proceedings by placing your dog on a leash and asking an adult whom the dog respects to hold the leash.

Allow your dog to gradually approach the rabbit's cage in a quiet manner. If the dog gets rambunctious, correct her by boldly saying "no" and quickly jerking the leash. When the dog approaches quietly, reward her with treats and praise to let her know that this is the kind of behavior that you expect when she is close to the rabbit.

When your rabbit first lays eyes on your dog, he will undoubtedly be frightened. He will probably dive into his nestbox and hide. Let him stay there, because that is where he will feel secure. Eventually, if the dog behaves in a nonthreatening manner, the rabbit will become braver and more curious, finally venturing out of the nestbox to investigate.

Once the dog and rabbit are comfortable with each other in this scenario, and once your rabbit is comfortable being out of his cage without the dog being present, you can try allowing them to come face-to-face without the cage. Begin by placing the dog on a leash. You may also want to muzzle her, just to be safe, and keep the treats handy.

Take your rabbit out of the cage and place him on a sofa or chair where he will be off the ground. (Don't place him too high, just in case he jumps off.) Stay next to the rabbit and reassure him with stroking and a soothing voice while the person holding the leash allows the dog to slowly approach. If the dog acts aggressively, correct her by saying "no" and jerking on the leash. If she nears the rabbit quietly to sniff him, reward her.

The rabbit, frightened by the dog's proximity and by being outside of his cage, may dart away. Your dog's first impulse will be to chase him. Teach the dog that this is not acceptable. Using her obedience training, issue the "sit" or "down" command so that she will come to understand that this is a "special" rabbit that must not be chased or harmed in any way.

Gradually allow more and more freedom between the two pets until they seem to be getting along well. (Muzzling your dog is highly recommended until you are completely confident that she will not harm the rabbit.) It may take as long as a few months for the animals to comfortably coexist, but if you are consistent, you should see results.

Keep in mind that some dogs, particularly those of the hunting breeds, no matter how hard their owners try, can never be taught not to chase or attack a rabbit. Their predatory instincts are simply too strong. In these cases, you will either have to keep the dog permanently separated from the rabbit, return the rabbit to his breeder or shelter, or take him to a foster home.

Cats

Cats are usually better companions for rabbits than dogs, primarily because the two species are similar in size. While cats are predators and are often inclined to chase rabbits, they are less capable of hurting the

Because they're similar in size, cats and rabbits usually make good companions.

bunny than are dogs, who can kill a rabbit with one snap of the jaw.

When preparing to introduce your cat and your rabbit, start out by buying a harness for your cat. Having your cat wear the harness during the no-cage introduction will give you control over her should she become combative. You should also have a water-filled squirt gun handy in case your cat gets rambunctious.

Using a nail trimmer, clip the claws on your cat's front paws. Should your cat become aggressive toward the rabbit, she will do little harm if her claws are dull.

Start out by showing the rabbit to your cat while the rabbit is still in his cage. The two animals will be very wary of each other at first, and the rabbit may hide in his nestbox.

If your cat approaches tentatively and does not behave aggressively toward the rabbit, reward her. If the cat hisses and runs away, ignore her. She will undoubtedly come back to investigate and will eventually get used to the intruder. If the cat reaches her paw into the cage and tries to get at the rabbit, squirt her with the water pistol from a distance. This will let her know that aggressive behavior toward the rabbit is not acceptable.

Once the two animals begin to ignore each other, you'll know that you are ready for the next step. Allow your rabbit out of his cage, with your cat on the harness. When the rabbit hops, the cat may move toward him as if to chase him. Don't allow this. Instead, keep the cat still and let her watch the rabbit move around the room until she gets used to the idea that she's not allowed to chase. You will need to repeat these getting-acquainted sessions on a regular basis until both animals are comfortable with each other. It may take some time, but in most cases your efforts will pay off.

Once the rabbit has had a chance to get used to the cat, he will probably learn to ignore her, but there is a chance he will behave aggressively when the cat comes too close.

If your rabbit does behave aggressively toward your cat, let your cat get away from the rabbit. A cat that feels threatened and cornered will strike out and possibly hurt the rabbit. If your rabbit repeatedly seeks out your cat and attacks her for no apparent reason, you will have to teach your rabbit not to behave this way. Use the squirt-gun method mentioned above to help the rabbit understand that inappropriate aggression toward other animals in the home is unacceptable.

Other Rabbits

Fostering cohabitation between two rabbits is even more complicated than encouraging it among a rabbit and a dog or cat. In the wild, rabbits live with their own kind in complex societies. Whenever a rabbit is introduced to a member of his own species, the two lagomorphs have to establish their position in their hierarchy.

The first step toward a successful friendship among rabbits is spaying and neutering. Hormone activity can cause an intact rabbit to fight with another rabbit with whom he might normally get along. Spaying and neutering eliminate hormones from the equation, making rabbits calmer and more docile with one another.

When deciding whether two rabbits will become friends, keep in mind that gender can be an important factor. Spayed females and neutered males tend to get along better than other gender combinations. In most situations, however,

---

RABBIT ESSENTIALS

hutch or cage

nestbox

food dish

water bottle

hay rack

food (pellets, hay, fresh greens)

litter box and litter

straw or wood shavings for bedding

chewing blocks

toys

travel carrier

slicker or pin brush

flea comb

nail trimmer

---

rabbits that are strangers will behave assertively toward each other, regardless of gender. This is why it is necessary to allow them to gradually get accustomed to one another.

Begin by finding a place of neutral territory, where neither rabbit has had a chance to stake a claim, such as a room in the house where neither has ever been. Placing the rabbits on unclaimed turf will temper their instinctive urge to defend territory against one another.

Keep the rabbits in their individual cages at first, and put the cages next to each other. Leave them together like this as often as possible. Once they seem comfortable with each other, you can place them together in the neutral territory while both are on harnesses. Keep them from getting too close to each other, but allow them to spend as much time together as possible.

Once their tensions have subsided and they seem less hostile toward each other, let them get a little closer together while still on their leashes. This way, if they do attack each other, you will have control and can separate them.

Eventually, you can allow them to run together in the neutral space. There might be some fighting, but you can break it up by squirting your water gun. The rabbits will eventually work it out between themselves and will learn to tolerate each other, or, hopefully, become fast friends.

CHAPTER THREE

Bunny Behavior

In order to have a rewarding relationship with your rabbit, it's important that you understand her. The domestic rabbit is very similar to the wild rabbit in the way that she behaves and communicates. The instincts you see expressed by your pet mimic those of rabbits in nature.

RABBIT BEHAVIOR

To understand rabbit behavior, you must first realize that rabbits are prey animals. In the wild, they live their entire lives on the lookout for larger animals that want to eat them. Each individual rabbit's ability to be alert, wary and quick is what keeps her alive.

Protective Instincts in the Wild

Wild rabbits have a number of behaviors that help them avoid predators. In fact, each behavior that rabbits possess is designed to help them survive in the wild. The habit of standing on hind legs is one of these behaviors. Rabbits use this posture to evaluate their surroundings and judge the safety of their whereabouts. A rabbit standing on her hind legs will use her senses of sight, hearing and smell to check out the neighborhood to see if any predators are lurking nearby.

The old adage "safety in numbers" applies to the wild rabbit, which lives in social groups, known as colonies, that can contain as many as fifteen individual rabbits. Life in a group provides the rabbit with several avenues of security. First, the more rabbits there are, the safer it is for each individual rabbit. For every rabbit that lives in the colony, there is another set of eyes scouring the landscape, on the lookout for enemies. When one rabbit spies a predator, she gives a signal to the others that danger is near.

The warren, a complex set of underground burrows created by the colony, provides another form of protection against predators. Because warrens consist of many different burrows, there is rarely a shortage of holes to dive into when an enemy approaches.

Another way that wild rabbits protect themselves from predators is to freeze and flatten their bodies against the ground. To a coyote or bobcat, the rabbit's agouti fur blends right into the foliage. This game of camouflage works well for the rabbit, which often goes unseen.

In the event that the camouflage doesn't work and the predator does attack, the rabbit is equipped with strong hindquarters to help her dash away. Sprinters by design, rabbits can reach speeds of up to 24 miles per hour over a short distance. They use this swiftness to get their lithe bodies to a hole or other place where they can hide.

Rabbit Social Hierarchy

In addition to their self-protection instincts, rabbits also live by a set of instinctual behaviors that allows them to live peacefully within their communities. Each rabbit colony contains a dominant male and a dominant female, with the other members of the group assuming various levels of dominance and submission below them. This social hierarchy contributes to the survival of the species; the strongest, most dominant animals are likely to out-live the lesser members of the colony and go on to reproduce.

Despite the differences in rank among individuals, the colony of rabbits works as a group to protect its territory from other intruding rabbits. Wild rabbits rarely venture far from the safety of the warren, and establish territories that they consider their own. Marking of this territory and fighting is common among wild rabbits, which must prevent other rabbits from encroaching upon their turf.

COMMUNICATING WITH YOUR RABBIT

In order to communicate with your rabbit and develop a good relation-ship with her, you need to under-stand how her instincts translate into behaviors displayed within the domestic environment you have created for your pet.

Your rabbit's body language can tell you a lot about what she thinks of her surroundings.

25

Easing Fears

Always remember that rabbits are prey animals and are easily frightened. When you sense that your rabbit is afraid, speak to her in a soft voice and move slowly when near her. This will help your rabbit distinguish you from an attacking predator, which would move quickly and aggressively.

Be Considerate and Consistent

Know, too, that your rabbit's ears are very sensitive. Designed to detect even the most subtle sounds of lurking predators, they are especially sensitive to the loud noises of a human environment. For this reason, noise should be kept to an absolute minimum. The kindest thing a rabbit owner can do is to create a quiet, soothing atmosphere for his or her pet.

Rabbits in the wild forage for food mostly in the early morning hours and during twilight. They create a regular schedule for themselves and stick to it. Given this, the most natural times for your rabbit to eat are in the morning and evening. Be consistent with your pet, providing her with her breakfast and dinner at the same time every day.

Keep in mind that young rabbits are different from older rabbits in their behavior and attitudes. Rabbits under 1 year of age have not reached their full maturity. This means they will often behave in a rambunctious manner, much like a puppy or kitten. Young rabbits tend to be particularly active when it comes to chewing, spraying and digging. Neutering or spaying can help to diminish these behaviors, but be prepared to be tolerant and understanding. Patience is the key to helping a rabbit get through this "teenage" period. A more mature and less troublesome adult will undoubtedly emerge with the passage of time.

Body Language

As you spend time with your rabbit, you will begin to notice that she has certain mannerisms and actions that may seem odd to you. Because rabbits communicate primarily with body language, most of the behaviors you witness are silent messages about how your rabbit feels about you and her environment.

CHIN RUBBING—If you have ever noticed your rabbit rubbing her chin on the corners of the furniture, the edges of her nestbox or on your hand, you are witnessing a display of territorial marking. The scent glands located on the underside of your rabbit's face leave an odor detectable to other rabbits. When another rabbit smells the odor, she will know that this particular territory belongs to the owner of that scent. A rabbit feels safest in territory she has marked.

EAR SHAKING—Many rabbits use their ears to express their dislike for something. If your rabbit smells something unpleasant or has had her fill of handling, she may shake her ears in an attempt to rid herself of whatever is annoying her. This is a cue to you that your rabbit is displeased.

FLATTENING—Wild rabbits flatten their bodies to avoid being seen by predators, as do pet rabbits. This stance is one of fear. If your rabbit assumes this position, reassure her that everything is okay and remove her from the situation that is frightening her.

LITTLE-KNOWN RABBIT FACTS

Did you know that your rabbit . . .

- can be trained?
- can be taught to use a litter box?
- can purr with her teeth?
- can be trained to walk on a leash?
- has constantly growing teeth?
- can jump up to 3 feet high?
- can be highly affectionate and loyal?
- will sometimes get the notion to play a game of tag with you?

27

KICKING—Rabbits engage in different types of kicking, depending on their mood. When a rabbit is being held incorrectly or feels insecure because of the way she is being lifted, she will kick ferociously in an effort to escape. Kicking is also used in play, especially by rabbits that are joyously running about.

LICKING—Rabbits lick for much the same reason that cats or dogs do: to show affection. Rabbits will groom one another with their tongues and will also "groom" their human friends as well. If your rabbit

Purring is a noise rabbits make when they are content, although it is different from a cat's purr. The sound of a rabbit's purr is created by her teeth. Clicking is a sound made by some rabbits after they eat something particularly tasty. Soft teeth grinding is a sound made by a happy rabbit, while loud teeth grinding is a sign of severe pain. Screaming is something rabbits do only when they are very frightened, usually when they are being attacked by a predator.

THUMPING—In the movie *Bambi*, a little gray rabbit named Thumper got his name by repeatedly stamping his back leg on the ground. This behavior is not just the stuff cartoons are made of. Real-life rabbits actually thump their hind legs on the ground whenever they want to issue a warning of some kind. You may see your rabbit do this under a variety of circumstances, usually when something has attracted her attention and made her uncertain.

A rabbit's grooming behaviors can be as endearing as they are efficient.

licks you, she is trying to tell you that she thinks that you are special.

SOUNDS—While rabbits are primarily silent creatures, bunnies do vocalize on occasion. A rabbit will hiss when she is feeling aggressive, usually toward another rabbit.

CHAPTER FOUR

Caring for Your Bunny

Rabbits are relatively easy pets to care for once you have taken the time to learn about their health requirements. While dogs, cats and humans all share a similar physiological makeup, rabbits actually have a great deal in common with horses in the way their bodies work. For this reason, you will have to make a concerted effort to learn about the dietary needs of your rabbit, which differ from the dietary needs of other pets and from your own.

FEEDING

What you feed your rabbit can mean the difference between a healthy, long-lived pet and a sickly, unhappy animal. Rabbits are herbivores; they eat only plant material. In nature, this characteristic causes the rabbit to be a grazer, or an animal that spends considerable amounts of time foraging for and eating plants. Because plant material is difficult to break down, the digestive tract of the rabbit is uniquely constructed.

It's important to give your rabbit a diet that simulates that which he would eat in the wild. Otherwise, your rabbit could develop chronic diarrhea or heart, liver or kidney disease. You do not want your rabbit to become obese, an affliction that veterinarians find to be the biggest health problem among domestic rabbits.

Pellets

Many people still believe that rabbits need to eat only pellets. This is a myth and is one of the reasons why there are so many overweight pet rabbits. While pellets are a valuable staple in a rabbit's diet, this type of food is not all a rabbit should be eating. Pelletized feed should make up only a small portion of what your rabbit eats.

When purchasing a pelletized rabbit feed, look for a product that contains at least 18 percent fiber.

The amount of food you give your rabbit each day should be determined by his age and size.

Read the packaging to be sure that the pellets are labeled "nutritionally complete."

Do not buy a large supply of pellets, because they do not remain fresh for extended periods. Purchase as much as your rabbit will consume in about a month. Storing them in the refrigerator will help keep them fresh.

QUANTITY

If your rabbit is young (under 8 months of age), you may leave a bowl of pellets in the cage at all times for him to eat at will. However, if you have an adult pet, you should only provide two feedings of pellets per day, as pellets are high in calories.

The size of your rabbit will determine how much pelletized feed you give him. If your pet is a dwarf or small rabbit weighing between 2 and 4 pounds, you should provide him with 1 ounce of pellets per day. If your small rabbit weighs between 5 and 7 pounds, 2 ounces are sufficient.

Medium-size rabbits weighing between 8 and 10 pounds can be fed 4 ounces per day. Large- and giant-breed rabbits that weigh in at 11 to 15 pounds can receive 6 ounces

daily. (Remember to split the number of ounces per day in half for each feeding.)

If your rabbit does not eat the pellets that you place in his dish, throw the old ration away before you refill the bowl. It's important for your rabbit to be offered only fresh pellets. Similarly, remember to wash out your rabbit's food dish frequently to prevent the buildup of bacteria that often develops in unwashed food containers.

Hay

When you purchased your rabbit's cage or hutch, you also bought a hay rack. The reason for this was that rabbits need free access to fibrous foods, and hay, which is pure roughage, fits the bill.

Hay can be obtained from a number of sources, including pet-supply stores, feed stores and local horse stables. When you purchase hay, check it for freshness. Good, clean hay should have a sweet smell and a minimum of dust. Examine it for mold, which can be very harmful to rabbits if ingested.

There are different types of hay available on the market. Your pet-supply store will stock packaged

FEEDING DO'S AND DON'TS

- Feed pellets to your rabbit, but don't feed them exclusive of other important foods, such as hay and greens.

- Avoid overfeeding, which can cause obesity.

- Store pellet feed in the refrigerator to maintain its freshness.

- Never feed your rabbit hay that shows signs of mold.

- Feed your rabbit two times a day and leave a handful of hay in the hay rack at all times.

- Wash your rabbit's food bowls frequently to avoid bacteria buildup.

- Feed your rabbit timothy hay, if available; if not, alfalfa hay is acceptable.

- Offer your rabbit fresh greens every day.

- Keep your rabbit's water bottle full at all times.

- Don't make abrupt changes in your rabbit's diet.

- Feed your rabbit treats, preferably fresh fruits, in moderation.

- Don't prevent your rabbit from eating the cecotropes produced by his large intestine; these are an important source of nutrients.

- Keep your rabbit's feeding schedule regular.

alfalfa and timothy hay, while feed stores and stables will stock baled hay. Timothy hay is generally the best choice for a bunny. If your rabbit is eating pellets, alfalfa hay is already included in his diet, and the addition of more alfalfa hay may cause him to become overweight. Hay cubes are not recommended for rabbits.

Give your rabbit a handful of fresh hay every day to keep his digestive system in good working order. Place the hay in the hay rack to help keep it from scattering all around the cage. Remove old hay from the cage and the rack before you replace it with new hay.

Greens

Fresh greens are another important dietary staple that should be provided daily.

Some of the best greens for rabbits include dark-leaf romaine lettuce, dandelions, carrot tops, broccoli, basil, spinach, celery and artichokes. Many other green leafy vegetables that humans eat are good for rabbits too, provided that the leaves are dark green in color.

Fresh, dark greens are an important part of your rabbit's daily diet.

33

Make sure that the greens you offer your rabbit are fresh, and be sure to wash them thoroughly to remove residual pesticides.

Treats

NATURAL TREATS—The healthiest treats to feed your rabbit are fresh fruits. Treats that rabbits enjoy include apples, pears, strawberries, peaches and tomatoes. While these items are particularly popular among rabbits, you can offer your pet just about any fruit. Just be sure to offer it in moderation.

COMMERCIALLY PREPARED TREATS—Commercially prepared treats can also be acceptable for rabbits, as long as the treats are offered sparingly. Avoid giving your rabbit commercial treats that contain sugar. Do not give your pet traditional human treats that are high in sugar or salt, including chocolate.

TWIGS AND BRANCHES—You may also want to occasionally provide some dried and aged twigs from an unsprayed fruit tree to your rabbit as a treat. Rabbits love to gnaw on branches and sometimes rip off the bark and eat it. (Finding twigs that are dried and aged is important, because some tree branches are poisonous when fresh.)

CECOTROPES—Several decades ago, researchers discovered that rabbits have an unusual way of supplementing their diet. Small, soft pellets known as cecotropes are produced by the rabbit's cecum (a part of his large intestine). These cecotropes, which contain special nutrients, pass from the anus and are then instinctively eaten by the rabbit. While this may seem very strange to us, nature developed this process as a way of aiding the rabbit's ability to absorb nutrients from the hard-to-digest cellulose material contained in plants.

In order for your rabbit to get the most nutrition from his diet, he must be able to consume an adequate amount of the cecotropes produced by his body. Because these pellets are usually ingested just as they leave the anus, you may see your rabbit eating them as they are produced. Do not try to discourage him from acting on this instinct, which usually takes place during the evening hours.

If for some reason your rabbit is not able to eat the cecotropes produced by his body, he could become seriously ill. Make sure your rabbit is provided with a solid place in his cage to sit—a cage floor constructed strictly of wire makes it difficult for a rabbit to consume his cecotropes.

OTHER ITEMS—While many pet-supply stores stock salt licks for use in rabbit cages, most rabbits do not need salt blocks if they are on a diet that includes pellets. Pellets that are nutritionally complete contain salt as a part of their ingredients. Providing a salt block cannot hurt your rabbit, however, and you can offer him one if he likes it.

Rabbits that are healthy and eating a balanced diet do not need vitamins added to their feed. Should your rabbit ever become ill or greatly stressed, your veterinarian may recommend a dietary supplement on a temporary basis, but you need not otherwise provide supplementation.

Water

Water is very important to maintain the health of a rabbit, and should be

Although your rabbit will groom himself quite often, an occasional brushing will do him good.

provided at all times. Many rabbits will drink nearly a quart of water a day. Change your rabbit's water daily and wash the water bottle out on a regular basis.

GROOMING

One of the first things you will notice when you start living with your rabbit is that he loves to groom himself. Rabbits are much like cats

in that respect and are always preening and primping.

However, there are some grooming tasks that you will need to take on for your rabbit. Because rabbits do shed, an overabundance of loose hairs can wind up in the animal's digestive tract, swallowed during the process of self-grooming. Grooming also provides you with a chance to look your rabbit over for any signs of parasites or ill health.

It is best to set aside an hour once a week for grooming. (Long-haired breeds must be groomed every day.) Using the tools you purchased, find a comfortable spot where you can sit with your rabbit on your lap.

Begin by brushing or combing your rabbit. If you notice that a lot of loose hairs are coming out, and it is spring or fall, your rabbit may be molting. A molting rabbit begins to lose much of his hair in preparation for the season to come. In the summertime, the hair falls out so the rabbit will have less coat. In the winter, the shedded hairs are replaced by denser fur that will help keep the animal warm. During the molting seasons, it is best to brush your pet at least every other day.

If your rabbit has long hair, you will need to use your brush to work out any mats that you may find in his coat. Regular and careful grooming will prevent mats from forming. Another option for longhaired rabbits is to have them shorn by a professional groomer.

Grooming Checklist

When you are brushing and combing your pet, keep an eye out for fleas. Rabbits are just as susceptible to fleas as dogs are, especially if they live or play outside. If you find fleas on your pet, contact your veterinarian for information on how to rid your rabbit of these pests. Your veterinarian can provide you with rabbit-safe chemicals designed to kill fleas and give you details on how to eliminate fleas from your rabbit's environment.

As you brush or comb your rabbit, keep an eye out for any lumps or sores on the animal's body that could be an indication of disease or infection. Crusts and scabs suggest the presence of mites.

While you are handling him, check your rabbit's eyes and ears for any discharge. Examine the bottoms of his feet for sores and check under his chin to make sure that his scent gland is not swollen or infected.

Your rabbit's ears should also be attended to during the regular grooming session. Examine them for signs of waxy buildup or debris. Clean your pet's ears of wax with a solution that can be purchased from your veterinarian. Dark wax or the appearance of dirt in the ears can be a sign of ear mites. Never stick cotton swabs or any such items into the ear canal.

If you own one of the lop-eared breeds, you will have to pay special attention to the ears during grooming time. Because an ear that hangs down instead of standing straight up is not natural and fosters moisture buildup, lop-eared rabbits are more prone to ear infections. Examine your lop's ears closely for excess wax buildup, debris or foul smell.

Trimming Nails

Trimming your rabbit's toenails is also a necessary part of your grooming sessions, although it will not need to be done every week. Check the length and condition of your rabbit's nails every time you groom him. Once they appear to be getting long, it is time to trim them.

Prepare to trim your rabbit's nails by wrapping him in a towel and placing him gently in your lap, with his legs facing upward. Use your clipper to take off a portion of the nail. Be careful not to cut the quick in the toenail, because doing so can cause pain to the rabbit and a bloody toenail. A silhouette of the quick can be seen by holding the nail up to a light.

If you are nervous about trimming your rabbit's nails, or if your

Check your rabbit's nails from time to time and trim them once they appear to have grown too long.

37

rabbit struggles when you try to hold him in your lap, you may want to ask your veterinarian to show you how to perform this necessary function safely and effectively before you do it yourself.

Avoid Bathing

Although you might be tempted, try to avoid giving your rabbit a bath. As a rule, rabbits don't enjoy being bathed and rarely need to be. If your rabbit needs his bottom cleaned, cleanse it with rabbit-safe shampoo and water without submerging the entire rabbit in water.

CHAPTER FIVE

To Good Health

R abbits that are well fed and properly cared for rarely get sick. However, if a rabbit's basic needs for a proper diet, a clean environment and regular exercise are not met, the animal will become susceptible to a number of dangerous illnesses.

In other words, taking good care of your rabbit will pay off in the long run. And, because many rabbit ailments are difficult to cure, prevention is the best policy.

DISEASE PREVENTION

If you follow the feeding and housing guidelines outlined in this book, your rabbit should live a long and healthy life. There are, however, extra precautions that you can take to ward off illnesses and ways to address problems effectively, should they arise.

Diet

Probably the single most important step to take in keeping your rabbit healthy is feeding her the proper diet. In order for the digestive system to work properly, your rabbit needs to eat certain foods. (See chapter 4 for more information on this subject.) A correctly functioning digestive system will help your rabbit ward off a number of ailments that often trouble less well kept animals.

When changing your rabbit's diet or adding a new food, do so gradually. A sudden alteration in your pet's diet can wreak havoc on her digestive system and cause her to become seriously ill.

It is also extremely important to see that your rabbit's diet contains an adequate amount of clean, fresh water. Dehydration can be a life-threatening condition in rabbits.

Cleanliness

An unsanitary cage is a breeding ground for disease. A number of different illnesses can be directly traced to dirty floors and nestboxes, and unclean food bowls and water bottles. Remove fouled bedding and fecal matter daily, and wash the cage or hutch once a week to keep the growth of bacteria to a minimum. Scrub out your rabbit's food dish and water bottle every day.

Stress

Rabbits are susceptible to stress just as humans are. Unlike most humans, however, your rabbit cannot do much to change her lifestyle and alleviate her stress. She relies on you to do this for her.

Stress has serious consequences on the body's immune system and a rabbit's stress should be kept to a minimum. This means that the animal should not be exposed to loud noises, constant handling (especially by children), severe temperature changes and situations that will cause her to be frightened.

FINDING A VETERINARIAN

Your bunny's body differs considerably from that of a cat or dog, and some of the treatments and medications appropriate for these other pets could be harmful to your rabbit. In light of the special needs of rabbits, it's important to use only a veterinarian who has experience in treating them.

Because veterinarians who specialize in treating rabbits may be harder to find than traditional small-animal doctors, it is wise to select your rabbit's veterinarian before she actually needs one.

The best way to find a rabbit veterinarian is by referral. Ask other rabbit owners who they use, and whether they are happy with this individual or clinic. Speak to the breeder or rescuer from whom you got your rabbit. If you don't know any other rabbit owners near you, contact the House Rabbit Society. (See chapter 12.) People there will be able to help you locate a rabbit veterinarian in your area.

Once you have selected a veterinarian, it's a good idea to take your new rabbit in for an examination. The veterinarian will be able to tell you if your pet has any potential health problems and will set up an appointment for a spay or neuter. This will also give you an opportunity to meet the doctor and start a

file on your rabbit. This is also a good time to ask the veterinarian to show you how to clip your rabbit's nails and to answer any questions that you may have on how to care for your new pet.

OBSERVATION

Get to know your rabbit and keep a close eye on her. If you know how she looks when she is healthy, you'll be more likely to recognize signs of illness early on. Many diseases that can be fatal are often curable in their earliest stages. Realizing that your rabbit is "under the weather" before she becomes seriously ill could be the key to her recovery.

Regular grooming is an important part of observation, as this hands-on procedure will encourage you to take a close look at your pet. The tasks required during regular grooming, such as maintenance of your pet's nails and regular brushing, are essential to preventing illness and injury.

Examine your rabbit's litter box regularly. Keep an eye out for diarrhea, lack of feces or passed hairballs—any of these events can indicate a possible problem.

If your rabbit exhibits any of these signs, contact your veterinarian immediately.

SPAYING/ NEUTERING

One of the leading causes of death in older female rabbits is uterine cancer. You can prevent this illness in your doe by having her spayed after the age of 4 months. Spaying, a removal of the internal female organs, also prevents breast cancer and other hormone-related illnesses.

If your rabbit is a male, neutering (removal of the testes) after the age of 4 months can help him stay healthy, as well. Unneutered male rabbits often become aggressive and frequently get injured in fights with rabbits and other pets. Males that have not been neutered often spray urine as a territorial marker, creating odorous messes for their owners to clean. Because neutering is a simple veterinary procedure, it is well worth the effort.

COMMON AILMENTS

There are quite a few illnesses that affect rabbits, but many are rarely seen. Below is a list of the most common health problems in pet rabbits today.

Your veterinarian will need to ask you questions about your rabbit's activities and lifestyle before he or she can treat her.

SIGNS OF ILL HEALTH

How will you know if your rabbit isn't feeling well? In addition to drastic changes in behavior, here are some tell-tale signs to watch for:

- dull look in the eyes
- lethargy
- loud teeth grinding
- loss of appetite
- constipation/diarrhea
- discharge from eyes or nose
- bloated abdomen
- labored breathing
- unexplained weight loss

Abscesses

Abscesses are bacterial infections that result from a puncture wound of some kind. If your rabbit has cut herself on something or has had a fight with another pet, she may develop an abscess at the site of the injury. You will recognize an abscess by its round appearance and the discharge and foul smell that usually accompany it. Your

veterinarian will treat your rabbit with antibiotics to rid her of the infection.

Coccidiosis

A very common illness in rabbits, coccidiosis is caused by protozoa that affect the digestive system. Symptoms include loss of appetite, diarrhea, poor coat quality, distended abdomen and weight loss. Coccidiosis is most often seen in rabbits that are kept in unsanitary cages. This disease is almost always fatal, and so it is important to keep your rabbit's cage as clean as possible.

Constipation/Diarrhea

Difficulty defecating (constipation) or a very loose stool (diarrhea) can be the result of either poor diet or illness. Symptoms that usually indicate constipation are straining during elimination, lack of feces in the litter box, distended abdomen and lethargy. Diarrhea is usually indicated by a loose or runny stool and a dirty tail. If you see evidence that your rabbit is experiencing either of these problems, take her to your veterinarian to have the problem assessed.

Fleas

The same fleas that attack dogs and cats also prey on rabbits. You'll know that your rabbit is plagued by a flea infestation if you find dark spots that resemble particles of black dirt in her fur. To verify that a particle is "flea dirt," place it on a paper towel and put a drop of water on it. If it turns red, then the particle is digested blood left on your pet by a flea. If your rabbit has light-colored fur, you may even see a few of these tiny pests hopping around on your animal's body.

Fleas can be treated in several different ways. The most effective method is to apply a rabbit-safe chemical to the pet while also applying another spray to the rabbit's environment. Your veterinarian can supply you with the proper products as well as detailed instructions on how to rid your rabbit of these pests.

Flies

Flies can be very dangerous to rabbits, particularly to those kept outdoors. Flies often lay their eggs on a rabbit's soiled rectal area, leaving maggots to burrow in and feed on the animal's flesh. They can be kept at bay by keeping both your rabbit's cage and her fur clean. If flies do lay eggs on your rabbit, contact a veterinarian for assistance.

Hairballs

Because rabbits are such voracious groomers, they frequently ingest large volumes of their own hair. Because bunnies cannot vomit, they must pass any hair that they swallow. If a rabbit is not getting enough roughage in her diet, this hair can cause intestinal blockages and eventual death. Signs of a hairball

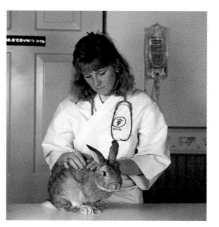

Running your hands over your rabbit's body daily is a good way to stay apprised of her physical condition.

Giving your rabbit a small amount of pineapple juice each month can help prevent hairballs.

problem include loss of appetite and masses of hair in the feces. Giving your rabbit a small amount of pineapple juice every month or so can help her with this problem, but it is a preventative measure, not a cure. If you think that your bunny may be suffering from ingestion of too much hair, consult your veterinarian.

Heat Prostration

Rabbits are very susceptible to overheating. When the weather is hot, keep a close eye on your pet. Signs of heat prostration include a stretched-out posture, panting, rapid breathing and foaming at the mouth. If you find your rabbit in this state, move her to a cool place out of the sun and place a cold, wet towel around her head. Offer her some fresh water. Heat prostration constitutes an emergency situation. Contact your veterinarian immediately.

Malocclusion

When a rabbit's front teeth do not wear down properly, the condition is known as malocclusion. This problem is usually inherited genetically. Signs of malocclusion include overly long teeth, infections in the mouth, ulcerations on the lips or tongue, jaw problems and difficulty eating. This is a common problem in rabbits, and must be handled by a veterinarian to prevent eventual death. Treatment consists of either regular trimming or complete removal of the teeth.

Mites

Rabbits are susceptible to two different kinds of mites: fur mites and ear mites. Fur mites cause patches of skin on the rabbit's body to become red and scabby. Clumps of hair are often missing. Ear mites settle in the rabbit's ear canals, causing itching and a dark, waxy discharge. Both of these mites are easily spread from one animal to another. Contact your veterinarian for information on how to treat either of these parasites.

Myxomatosis

Myxomatosis is a sort of rabbit plague. Spread deliberately throughout Europe in the 1800s to kill off large populations of wild rabbits, the disease still exists today. Mostly found in coastal California and Oregon, myxomatosis causes swelling around the eyelids, ears and nose, and a high fever. Nearly always fatal, this virus is spread by mosquitoes and biting flies. If you live in an area where myxomatosis is common in wild-rabbit populations, it might be wise to keep your pet indoors.

Obesity

Veterinarians report that obesity is the biggest health problem that they

If your rabbit's teeth don't wear down properly, you'll have to have them trimmed to prevent problems.

see in rabbits. Rabbits that are over-weight are prone to a number of ill-nesses that affect major organs. The primary cause of obesity in rabbits is the overfeeding of pellets. Rabbits that are obese should be placed on a special diet to help them get down to their proper weight.

Pastuerellosis

Also known as "snuffles," this com-mon bacterial disease affects the rabbit's respiratory system. Characterized by sneezing and coughing, along with wet and matted fur on the front legs, pastuerellosis is highly contagious and should be treated with antibiotics.

Ringworm

Ringworm, which also affects humans, cats, dogs, horses and other animals, causes dandruff and fur loss on rabbits. Ringworm is highly con-tagious, and immediate treatment by a veterinarian is recommended.

Sore Hocks

Rabbits that live in cages with wire floors often develop sore hocks. This condition is typified by red, swollen skin on the hind legs with accompa-nying hair loss. A veterinarian will provide an antibiotic ointment for treatment and will recommend a change in cage flooring.

Wet Dewlap

When a rabbit repeatedly dips her head into a bowl of water, a condition called wet dewlap can result. Infection often occurs in the dewlap, chin and front legs because the skin in these areas is nearly always wet. Does are especially prone to this disease, as their dew-laps are considerably larger than those of bucks.

Wet dewlap should be treated by a veterinarian, who will prescribe either an antibacterial or antifungal ointment, depending on the nature of the infection. This ailment can be prevented with the use of a gravity water bottle instead of a water bowl.

Worms

Roundworms and tapeworms, two parasites that commonly afflict dogs, also prey on rabbits. Symptoms of worm infestation include a distended abdomen, poor coat condition and worms in the litter box or near the anus. To prevent your rabbit from contracting these parasites, keep her away from outdoor areas where dogs defecate. If you suspect that your rabbit has worms, contact your veterinarian.

CHAPTER SIX

Indoor Bunnies

It's impossible to truly appreciate life with a rabbit unless you keep him inside your home. Just like a dog or a cat, rabbits are companion animals with personalities all their own. If you don't actually live with a rabbit, day in and day out, you'll never get to know him as well as you could—nor will he get to know you.

There are also many practical reasons for keeping a rabbit indoors. Rabbits that live inside tend to live longer than outdoor rabbits. Illness is a significant cause of death in outdoor rabbits, as it is more difficult to monitor their health. Signs of sickness can be subtle at first, and it can be a day or so before illness is even recognized.

HOUSING

Even though your indoor rabbit will have a roof over his head in a literal sense, he'll still need his own private retreat. A cage can offer security for your rabbit and can also offer him privacy and a safe haven. Cages are useful during litter-box training and while your rabbit is learning to behave himself around the house.

Indoor rabbit cages are readily available in a wide variety of styles in pet-supply stores and through catalogs. When searching for just the right cage for your indoor rabbit, look for one made from sturdy wire with a removable bottom tray. Your rabbit will not gnaw on the wire, and the removable tray will make cleaning easier. Wire will also allow your pet to receive the ventilation and light that he needs while confined.

Look for a cage that is well constructed and easy to disassemble for cleaning. The cage should have a door on top so that you can reach inside. It should also have a door on the side so that the rabbit can go in and out of the cage on his own.

The mesh on the cage wire (top and sides) should be no more than 1 by 2 inches in size, because anything larger is dangerous to your rabbit. A leg or head could get caught in mesh that is too big.

Cage Flooring

If your indoor rabbit will be litter-box trained, there is no need for the traditional wire mesh floor usually seen in outdoor hutches. In this case, the floor of the indoor rabbit cage can be solid, made of either rustproof metal or hard plastic. A solid floor is useful if you choose not to provide your pet with a nestbox, because it can also accommodate loose bedding such as straw, shavings or a blanket.

It is acceptable for indoor rabbit cages to have wire flooring, if this is the style that you prefer. Make sure the wire is galvanized with the

49

ADVANTAGES OF INDOOR HOUSING

- You can train your rabbit to use a litter box and avoid cleaning a large outdoor hutch.

- You get to know your pet's personality better when you spend more time with him.

- Your rabbit will be a constant companion, not just an outdoor pet.

- You don't have to worry about the effects of inclement weather on your rabbit's health and well-being.

- Because it's easier to monitor your rabbit's health when he's indoors with you, indoor rabbits live longer than those kept outside.

Your rabbit's cage and litter box will both need regular cleanings.

smooth side down. The mesh should be about 1 by ½ inches in size. Wire is uncomfortable for a rabbit's feet, and prolonged time on wire floors can result in sore hocks. For this reason, a piece of wood (any type except redwood, which is toxic to rabbits) should be placed in the cage to give the rabbit a place to sit off the wire.

Cage Size

If your indoor rabbit will spend a lot of time loose in the house and not in his cage, he will not need as big an enclosure as would his outdoor counterpart. Even if this is the case, the indoor cage should still be big enough for the rabbit to stretch out and hop around in while also accommodating a small litter box, an area for sleeping far from the litter box, food and water accessories and a toy or two. The height of the cage should also allow the rabbit to stand up on his hind legs without his ears touching the top. If you plan to include a nestbox, be sure the cage is tall enough to hold the box.

If your rabbit is very young, you may want to consider buying a smaller cage, because indoor rabbit cages are relatively inexpensive. You can then purchase a bigger one later on when your rabbit is fully grown (at about 6 months of age, depending on the breed).

Nestboxes

A nestbox is a small boxlike enclosure with an entry hole cut into it that contains the animal's bedding, and provides a safe place for the rabbit to sleep and hide. A cardboard box can work as a nestbox, but because most rabbits will chew a cardboard nestbox to pieces, a wood nestbox is preferable. Commercially made nestboxes are available through pet-supply outlets and mail-order catalogs that specialize in rabbit supplies, or you can build your own nestbox.

Your rabbit's nestbox should be big enough for the animal to turn around in while several inches of bedding (straw or wood shavings) are in place. Make sure the entrance to the nestbox is big enough for your rabbit to gain entry, and that one side of the box is removable so that you can clean it.

Cage Location

When determining where in the house to place your rabbit's cage, remember that heat is an extremely dangerous element for rabbits. Do not put your rabbit's cage in a spot where the sun will shine directly on it, and avoid keeping it near a radiator, stove, fireplace or other heating element.

While heat is hazardous to a rabbit's health, cold drafts can also be deadly. Keep your rabbit's cage away from doors and windows, where winter drafts can leak in through joints. Try to keep your rabbit's cage off the floor during cold weather, too, as cold air tends to lie near the ground, creating drafts.

Avoid placing your rabbit's cage in dark and damp areas. Basements and garages are not usually suitable areas for bunnies—these places in the home typically have minimal light, poor ventilation and excess moisture. Garages are also dangerous because rabbits are sensitive to automobile exhaust.

Try to find a place in your home where your rabbit will be able to watch household activity without being unduly disturbed. You want your rabbit to feel like part of the family, so his cage needs to be in a room where people come and go. However, don't put him in such a busy spot that he will never be able to rest or relax.

RABBIT-PROOFING

Because rabbits are gnawing mammals and have an innate need to chew, it is vitally important that you rabbit-proof your home before you let your rabbit run loose.

It's great to let your rabbit roam safe areas of the house, but you must first remove potential sources of danger and troublemaking.

52

Electrical Cords

Electrical cords pose the greatest threat to the safety of your rabbit, and should be of primary concern. Rabbits can and will chew through electrical cords, risking the chance of electrocuting themselves and causing a fire hazard in your home. You can protect your home and your rabbit by moving dangling cords up out of reach. Cords that cannot be moved should be covered with plastic aquarium-type tubing: Slit the tubing lengthwise and put the cord inside of it. Or, you can try wrapping the cord with spiral cable wrap available in electronics stores.

Wooden Surfaces

Wooden corners and other chewable areas that will be attractive to your rabbit can be covered with thick plastic or treated with an odoriferous substance. Perfume and cologne are very repugnant to rabbits, which have a sharp sense of smell. Store-bought repellents designed to deter other pets can also be used. Not all rabbits will be rebuffed by unpleasant odors, however, and you may have to resort to covering problem areas with an unchewable surface.

Digging

In addition to being compulsive chewers, rabbits are also vehement diggers. One way your rabbit may choose to express his digging instinct will be to assail your carpeting. He'll find a spot where the carpet separates from the wall and proceed to dig it up. He may even chew on the fibers, which could prove disastrous to his digestive tract.

Encourage your rabbit to excavate elsewhere by providing him with a box of soil that he can dig in to his heart's content. Place the box in the bathtub or other area of the house where the dirt won't fly everywhere. Then, when your rabbit begins to tunnel through the carpet, gently pick him up and place him in the box of dirt. You can also try firmly tacking the carpeting down and treating it with an odorous repellent to discourage him from returning to that area.

Nooks, Crannies and Other Hazards

Another important part of rabbit-proofing your home is taking a survey of all the places where your

rabbit could get caught or hide. Rabbits are very inquisitive animals, and you can be sure that your pet will explore every nook and cranny of your house. Look around for rabbit-size spaces through which your pet could escape or in which he could get trapped. Block these areas up securely. While you're busy

Covering your electrical cords with plastic tubing is wise; rabbits need to chew and cords are a common target.

surveying the house, make sure that toxic household chemicals and trash bags are well hidden from your pet.

LITTER-BOX TRAINING

One of the reasons that rabbits make excellent indoor pets is their receptivity to litter-box training. The rabbit's denning instinct, which he inherited from his wild ancestors, is responsible for this inherent behavior. Rabbits, just like cats and dogs, prefer not to foul the area where they eat and sleep and will instead venture out of their "dens" to relieve themselves.

Some rabbits are easily trained to use the litter box, while others require more time and patience. The most important things to remember when litter-box training a rabbit are consistency and praise. Never scold your rabbit for not using the litter box, because this will only frighten and confuse him. Another important point is to work gradually, starting your rabbit out in a small space and then moving up to giving him run of the whole house.

Most rabbit owners use organic cat litter for their rabbit's litter box, especially brands made from paper, wheat, grass and other organic materials. Stay away from clay- and

Rabbits are quite receptive to litter-box training.

wood-based litters, as these tend to be dusty and can cause respiratory problems in bunnies. Some pet-supply stores specializing in rabbits will carry litter made just for them, and this variety is the best type to buy. You can also use straw on top of a layer of newspaper as litter, although it will be less absorbent than most commercially made brands.

Start the litter-box training process in a very small area, preferably the rabbit's cage. Place a small litter box (the same type used for cats) in a corner of your rabbit's cage, attached to the side with a clip or twistable wire for removal when cleaning. Try to place the box in the area of the cage that your rabbit tends to use most frequently for elimination. Put some fecal pellets in the box to help give him the right idea and then add a handful of hay to a corner of the box to encourage him to use it.

Moving Beyond the Cage

Once your rabbit seems to be using the litter box in his cage and has been allowed to do so for some time, you can then try giving him a little more space. Create a special part of the house just for him. (Kitchens, bathrooms or hallways work best.) Use a baby gate to section off a small area so you can keep an eye on your rabbit.

Place the litter box in the small area, along with the rabbit's food, water and bedding. Watch your rabbit to make sure that he uses the litter box on a regular basis. If he is using the litter box successfully, then you can increase the amount of space in the house that is accessible to him.

If your rabbit starts making mistakes at any point in the process, he may not have been ready to make the transition to a larger area.

Giving your rabbit proper items to chew on, like these sugar maple twigs, will help keep him from chewing on furniture.

55

Return him to his cage and start over. Or, you may want to try buying a few more litter boxes and placing them in various parts of the rabbit's space. With so many litter-box options to choose from, he is bound to get the right idea. You can then try gradually removing all of the boxes except one. In the meantime, clean up after your pet by picking up fecal pellets with a tissue, and washing urine marks on carpeting with a mixture of vinegar and water. Urine on wood floors can be cleaned with simple soap and water.

Litter-Box Cleaning

When it's time to clean your rabbit's litter box (once or twice a week), use a water and vinegar solution, and dry it thoroughly before filling it with litter and returning it to its usual spot.

CHAPTER SEVEN

Outdoor Bunnies

If keeping your rabbit indoors is out of the question, it is possible to house your rabbit outside successfully if you take strict precautions. Before you prepare to bring your outdoor rabbit home with you, be sure to check your local zoning ordinances to make sure it is legal to keep a rabbit outdoors in your area.

HOUSING

When determining what kind of housing you will provide for your rabbit, and where it will be located, there are many details you must keep in mind in order to keep your rabbit healthy and safe.

Your first concern is the weather. You must protect your rabbit from the elements, as well as from extreme changes in temperature. You will also need to guard against predators, and allow your rabbit enough room to move around comfortably.

THE HUTCH

There are a number of commercially made hutches available on the market that are specifically designed for rabbits. It's important to choose a hutch that will meet your rabbit's needs for shelter, comfort and safety.

ADVANTAGES OF OUTDOOR HOUSING

- Litter-box training isn't necessary.

- You don't have to address urine spraying inside the house.

- Your rabbit can watch outdoor activity and be stimulated even when no one in the family is home.

- You don't run the risk of your rabbit chewing on your walls and furniture or digging in your floors or carpeting.

- Your rabbit doesn't have to get along with your other pets.

Size

First, consider size. The more room you can provide for your rabbit, the better. Buy your rabbit the largest hutch that your allotted space will accommodate.

When determining a suitable living space for a rabbit, keep your pet's size in mind. If you will be bringing home a baby or immature rabbit, find out how big she will grow to be.

A good rule of thumb when determining the minimum living room your rabbit will need is to calculate 1 square foot of space for each pound of rabbit. For example, a 9-pound Rex needs at least 9 square feet of cage space (3 feet by 3 feet). However, it is preferable to give your rabbit even more room than this. A rabbit that does not have enough room in her hutch may become depressed. Too small a space will also be fouled more quickly with feces and urine, leaving the rabbit to spend more time than she should in unsanitary conditions. On the other hand, don't get a single-door hutch that is so deep that you can't reach into it to clean it. Large hutches should have more than one access door.

You'll also want to make sure that your hutch is large enough to accommodate a separate sleeping space, either in the form of a nest-box or a built-in compartment. Providing your rabbit with a secluded and separate place to sleep will help her feel safer and happier in her hutch. A built-in sleeping compartment should be about $1\frac{1}{2}$ feet long and $\frac{1}{2}$ foot in height and width for small rabbits; $2\frac{1}{2}$ feet long and around 9 inches in height and width for medium-size rabbits and 2 feet long and about 1 foot in height and width for large rabbits.

Materials

Most rabbit hutches are made from either wood and wire or just wire. Each type has its advantages and disadvantages.

Wooden rabbit hutches usually consist of a wooden roof and several wood-panel sides, with wire mesh on the door, front and/or some sides of the cage. Wooden hutches stay cooler in the summer and warmer in the winter, provided that they are made with a good quality wood and not pressboard. They also can be very attractive.

However, because wood exposed to the elements is prone to rotting, the hutch will likely fall apart after some time. Another disadvantage to wood is that rabbits love to chew on it and can gnaw sections of a wooden hutch to pieces if the wood is not protected by wire mesh. Be sure, too, that the wood used is untreated, as treated wood can be toxic to a bunny that loves to chew. Some experts also believe that cedar can be toxic to rabbits and other small animals.

Metal hutches, on the other hand, have the disadvantage of retaining heat in the summer and cold in the winter, both of which can be harmful to the rabbit. Metal hutches are very durable, however, and can last a very long time if they are well made. They are also easier to clean than wood hutches and are frequently less expensive.

Hutch Specifications

Whether you choose a wooden hutch or a wire hutch, it's important to select a home for your rabbit that utilizes the proper type of wire. Chicken wire is not acceptable, as it is flimsy and easily removed by both the rabbit and by predators. Side panels and doors on both wooden and metal hutches should be made from sturdy, galvanized wire, around 14 gauge in weight. The size of the holes in the wire mesh should be no larger than 1 by 2 inches.

The roof of an outdoor hutch should be covered with a waterproof substance, such as heavy-duty plastic or roofing material. This is vital if the hutch and its occupant are to stay warm and dry in inclement weather.

Floor materials are very important in a hutch. Improper flooring can cause your rabbit to develop a number of health problems. Most hutches have some wire flooring, designed to allow feces and urine to drop down away from the rabbit. However, wire mesh that is too large can be dangerous, because the rabbit's foot may fall through the mesh. The wire mesh should also be smooth, as a rough edge can result in sore hocks.

With these issues taken into consideration, it is best to get a hutch with a floor made of $1/2$-inch-by-1-inch, 14-gauge, welded wire. Last but not least, make sure that at least one-third of the floor space contains a flat, porous surface (preferably wood) where your rabbit can sit to get off the wire.

Design

When considering which hutch to purchase for an outdoor rabbit, the factors of rabbit health, safety and comfort mentioned above obviously come into play. Beyond this, however, the choice of design of a hutch is a matter of individual preference based on convenience, quality and aesthetic appeal.

Quality

The first feature to look for in hutch design is quality. Does the hutch appear to be well built? Is it made from quality materials? Look to see that the welding was done before the metal was galvanized. Check the hinges and various connections throughout the hutch to determine whether they are well put together. Examine the construction carefully to make sure that the hutch is secure and escape-proof. Feel around the hutch for sharp points. Unfinished edges indicate sloppy handiwork and a potential danger to your rabbit.

Height

Another element to consider is height. Some hutches are made low to the ground, while others have legs that put them anywhere from several inches to several feet off the ground. It's always best, in the interest of better ventilation and sanitation, if the hutch is at least 6 inches off the ground. Hutches that rest directly on the soil invite rodents to nest underneath the floor. So, if you purchase a hutch with no legs, keep in mind that you'll have to create some means of elevating it to allow air to pass underneath.

If you do buy a hutch with legs, it is best if the legs raise the hutch to waist height. This kind of hutch is far easier to clean and allows easier access to the rabbit. In addition, unless you do decide to get a hutch that is particularly low to the ground, avoid models with a top-opening door and opt for the kind with a door in the front. This will also help you clean the hutch and access the rabbit with more convenience.

To ensure that the hutch fits the needs of their pet, many rabbit owners will actually design and build their own outdoor hutches. If you choose to do this, you may want to

While wooden hutches are frequently more attractive, metal hutches are more durable.

contact your local county extension office or the American Rabbit Breeders Association for plans and further information on how to construct a safe and sturdy hutch. (See chapter 12 for more information on how to contact ARBA.)

Location

TEMPERATURE AND

SUNLIGHT—Heat is more dangerous to rabbits than cold, so when choosing a location for your hutch, make sure it is in a shady spot. Temperatures above 80°F are considered dangerous for rabbits, especially if accompanied by high humidity. On the other hand, you don't want to keep your rabbit in total darkness, either. Pick a location with moderate sun exposure, but one in which the rabbit has sufficient shade all day long to keep her out of direct sunlight.

While bunnies are better able to tolerate cold than heat, they should still be protected from drafts, as well as from dampness. Constant wind or drafts are likely to cause your rabbit to get sick; hot, humid weather can cause moldy, unsanitary conditions in the nestbox; rain or snow can drench a rabbit and her entire bed. Choose a protected location for your rabbit hutch where it is out of drafts

A nestbox inside her hutch gives your rabbit a place to escape from heat and direct sunlight.

and wind. Placing it alongside a building can often provide defense from the wind.

Aside from keeping the rabbit away from direct sunlight and from taking her indoors, one way to protect your rabbit from overheating in the summertime is to provide her with plastic jugs of frozen water that she can lay against to keep cool. Keep a few of these jugs on hand in your freezer so you can rotate them once the ice melts.

VENTILATION—Ventilation is also an important factor in hutch placement. Caged rabbits need plenty of fresh air because a stuffy environment can wreak havoc on a rabbit's respiratory system. The ammonia from the rabbit's urine and the dust from her bedding can cause respiratory distress and infection, causing the rabbit to become sick and even die. Make sure you select a spot that, while still protected from the elements, is well ventilated.

PEACE AND QUIET—Also in the interest of the rabbit's well-being, don't place your hutch in a place where there is excessive noise. Rabbits like to nap during the day and will become nervous and stressed if there are frequent loud noises or disturbances.

CONVENIENCE AND SECURITY—When choosing a spot for your rabbit's home, keep in mind that you will need to have convenient access to it so you can clean it regularly, feed your rabbit and take her out daily for exercise and companionship.

It's also important to keep in mind that rabbits are prey animals and will attract any number of predators. Dogs and cats are only two of the creatures that will be drawn to your yard once a rabbit is in residence. Depending on where you live, raccoons, coyotes and even weasels may try to invade your rabbit's hutch.

Rabbit cages can be kept on apartment terraces as long as the space is protected just as it would be in a backyard. Provide shade for the hutch and safeguards from climbing predators, as well as protection from drafts and temperature extremes.

OUTDOOR RABBIT CARE

Rabbits that are housed outdoors need special attention. The most important aspect of outdoor rabbit care is observation. Because your rabbit is outside, you must be devoted to making time to spend with her every day.

As is true with humans, the early treatment of an illness can often mean the difference between life or death to a rabbit. Learn to recognize how she behaves when she is feeling well so you will immediately be aware when there is a problem.

Exercise

It's important that your rabbit receive daily exercise. If you cannot bring her inside the house to play,

then you'll have to provide her with a completely enclosed run in the backyard to stretch her legs. The run should be as big as possible, with 6 feet being the minimum length for a medium-size rabbit. If your yard is enclosed by walls or a sturdy fence with no holes that a rabbit can slip through, you may give her the run of the yard. However, a rabbit should never run loose without supervision as she may fall victim to a predator or poisonous plants in your yard. Because rabbits are excellent diggers, it's even possible that your rabbit may dig a tunnel right out of your yard if you're not watching her.

Social Interaction

Rabbits are highly social creatures, and an outdoor rabbit living alone in a hutch can suffer terribly from loneliness. For this reason, you will need to make a concerted effort to provide her with social interaction. Bring her in the house as often as you can so that she can spend time with you. Sit out in the backyard with her as she plays in her run or in the yard. And if you don't have a lot of time to do this, get another rabbit to keep her company in her hutch.

If you're not able to bring your outdoor rabbits inside to exercise, it's important that you have an enclosed run for them to use outside.

Regular Cleaning

Outdoor hutches get dirty quickly, and for your rabbit's health and well-being, you'll need to clean her hutch frequently. Although you need not clean it every day, it wouldn't hurt to do so. Time spent cleaning the hutch is also a good opportunity to inspect the inside of the structure for damage.

Before you clean the hutch, remove your rabbit and put her in a safe place. (A travel carrier is useful for this purpose.) Don't let her roam about unsupervised, as she may get into trouble while you are working.

Because rabbits normally live in dens, they tend to pick a specific area of their hutch to use for elimination. Using a spatula and hand shovel, scrape away the feces and urine that have built up in that area. Once a week, you should also scrub the area with a hard bristle brush and water mixed with a splash of bleach. Wait until the inside of the hutch is completely dry before placing the rabbit back in it.

Remember that outdoor rabbits require the same daily care that indoor rabbits do.

CHAPTER EIGHT

Fun with Bunny

Although many people think rabbits are boring creatures that do nothing but sit in a cage all day, those who live closely with rabbits know that this assumption is wrong.

Rabbits have gained a reputation in the past as uninteresting animals because, until recently, they were primarily kept as outdoor pets and received little human contact. Nowadays, however, many people have begun keeping their rabbits inside the house where the animals can interact with people and other pets. Even many outdoor rabbits

now get to spend some time indoors, roaming through the house and joining in the day's activities with their humans.

Given the rabbit's newfound opportunity to show us what he's all about, it's not surprising that people are discovering what a unique and fascinating pet he really is.

PLAYING

In the wild, rabbits are playful creatures that love to engage their fellow rabbits in games. R.M. Lockley, researcher and author of *The Private Life of the Rabbit,* observed wild rabbits chasing each other, running in circles, jumping into the air and rolling in the grass. In the situations Lockley observed, there was no reason for this behavior other than the fact that the rabbits felt good and wanted to show it.

Much like their wild ancestors, pet rabbits also like to play. Rabbits have been known to play with dogs and cats, as well as with other rabbits. They're even likely to play with humans if the game is right. Rabbits also love to amuse themselves with toys.

When it comes to interactive play with a rabbit, the decision of which game to play is best left up to the rabbit. Bunnies have been known to initiate games of tag with humans, to play "bat the ball" and to chase toys being dragged around in a circle. Because of their wary nature, a game of chase initiated by a human will usually frighten a rabbit that may suddenly feel like he is being preyed upon. However, if your rabbit starts to chase you, he either wants you to leave the area, or he is trying to play tag with you!

The best way to enjoy a rabbit at play is to give him a toy and then sit back and watch. Rabbits love to frolic around with a favorite toy, and their antics can be quite amusing. Playtime is beneficial for them too, both physically and emotionally.

TOYS

There are a number of toys you can provide for your rabbit. Store-bought toys made especially for rabbits are usually made from wood and can be batted about and then chewed on for hours. You can also amuse your rabbit with more readily available cat toys, including small rubber balls, plastic balls with bells in them and stuffed socks. If you do decide to offer your rabbit such toys, be sure not to let him chew them. Swallowing a piece of plastic or fabric can be harmful to a rabbit.

There are a number of household items that make excellent toys for rabbits. Try offering your pet a paper cup, an empty soda can, a small towel, a toilet paper spool, a cardboard box, straw baskets, a can with a penny or stone inside of it or a paper grocery bag. Alternate your rabbit's toys so he doesn't get bored with them.

TRAVELING

Because new situations often cause stress and anxiety in rabbits, and because new environments can mean exposure to disease and parasites, it's usually best to leave your pet at home while traveling. Ask a knowledgeable friend to take care of the rabbit, or hire a professional pet sitter to care for him while you're gone.

While some rabbits do not respond well to traveling, others enjoy the chance to get out of the house once in a while. If you take the proper precautions, you should be able to give your pet a change of scenery while still keeping him healthy.

Traveling by Airplane

Airplane rides are not recommended for rabbits unless absolutely necessary. If you are planning to fly somewhere, your rabbit would be better off left at home. Airplane travel is difficult for rabbits because most pets must travel in the plane's cargo hold, where temperatures are not often controlled. Pets frequently die of heatstroke while a plane sits on the runway waiting to take off, or from cold while the plane is high in the atmosphere.

Although some airlines do allow pets in the cabin of the aircraft, they must be kept in a pet carrier and placed underneath the seat in front of yours. Only very small rabbits will fit in these carriers, and even those rarely do so comfortably. All in all, the benefits of bringing your rabbit along on your vacation are probably not great enough to justify the stress your pet will encounter while traveling by air.

Traveling by Car

Rabbits can ride comfortably in cars when the day is cool and the traffic is minimal. If you must spend a significant amount of time sitting in traffic, try to keep the windows rolled up. Rabbits are sensitive to car exhaust.

If you want to find out if your bunny is the adventurous type that enjoys travel, you'll first need to get him used to the idea of riding in the car and being out of his usual surroundings.

Start by leaving his travel carrier in a place where he can have as much access to it as possible. Rabbits feel most secure in small enclosures, and you'll find that your rabbit will like to spend time in his carrier. Placing some hay in it will encourage him to visit the carrier often.

Using a Harness and Leash

In the meantime, work on getting your bunny used to wearing a harness and walking on a leash. Begin by putting his harness on him and letting him hop around the house under supervision. Once he seems at ease wearing the harness, you can then snap a leash on it and walk around the house with him.

Keep in mind that you will not be able to walk your rabbit in the same way that you would walk a dog. Rabbits cannot be taught to walk beside you or do most of the other things that leash-trained dogs do. Instead, your rabbit will hop around, and you will basically follow him. Always be gentle with your rabbit while walking him. If you need to get from one place to another while he is on the leash, pick him up and carry him there.

When your rabbit is comfortably walking on his harness, try taking him outdoors with it. Let him explore your backyard or another

Believe it or not, your rabbit can be trained to walk on a leash.

safe area, taking care not to allow him to eat any unknown plants or walk through areas that may have been sprayed with pesticides or visited by dogs.

Eventually, you'll be able to walk your rabbit out on the street or in a nearby park. Remember that your pet is vulnerable when he is outside of his home. It's up to you to keep an eye out for loose dogs that would love nothing more than to give chase to your bunny. Be sure never to leave your rabbit unattended or tied to anything, as he could become tangled in his leash and might panic. You will notice that your "rabbit on a leash" will get you a lot of attention from passersby and will be the subject of many impromptu conversations.

Bring Along a Bit of Home

Remember to bring along some of your rabbit's necessities. A supply of his regular food is a must, as is fresh hay, which should be placed in his carrier for him to munch on. His water bottle and a jug of the water you usually give him are also necessary. (Providing him with familiar water will ensure that he drinks as much as he needs.) Be sure to bring his litter box, too, so he can use it

Rabbits don't always enjoy the stresses of traveling, but if you choose to take your pet on a trip, make sure you take along some of the comforts of home.

once you arrive at your destination. Try to adhere to your normal schedule of feeding so as not to disrupt your rabbit's system.

SHOWING

Quite a few people who start out as casual pet owners eventually start showing their rabbits. Showing is a fun activity in which the entire family can participate. People who begin by simply showing a pet often become very involved in the activity and eventually acquire a number of rabbits.

If you and your family want to investigate the world of rabbit shows, you may first want to look into 4-H, an organization created to help children learn how to care for and exhibit livestock. The American Rabbit Breeders Association (ARBA), the official organization for rabbit showing, is another group that sponsors rabbit shows around the country. These shows are attended by rabbit fanciers who take the sport of showing quite seriously.

4-H

Shows specifically for 4-H rabbit owners are held around the country. These shows follow the rules and breed standards established by ARBA. 4-H members can also exhibit their rabbits at county fairs, as 4-H often has a strong presence at these events.

Open to children aged 9 to 19 (and sometimes even younger, depending on the individual club), typical 4-H rabbit projects feature hands-on learning in a family environment. Children are taught how to feed, care for, handle, groom and show their rabbits.

Rabbits are playful creatures that enjoy interaction with their owners.

ARBA

The American Rabbit Breeders Association, which began in the early part of the twentieth century, is the governing body for rabbit showing and registration in the United States. ARBA sanctions rabbit shows around the country. These shows, sponsored by regional rabbit clubs, are occasionally open to only one breed, but are often open to all breeds of rabbits.

ARBA has created a list of rules and regulations for rabbit shows, and each sanctioned show operates by these rules. Judges who officiate at ARBA shows evaluate the rabbits that they judge using the breed standards published by ARBA. Rabbits that are exhibited at ARBA shows may be registered with the organization (more information on how to register follows in this chapter), but doing so is not mandatory.

Rabbits at ARBA shows are judged in classes organized by breed. Within the breed classification, rabbits are then divided by age before they are judged. Awards are given to individual class winners, as well as Best of Breed, Best of Opposite Sex (given to the best rabbit of the sex opposite the Best of Breed winner), Best of Variety or Group and ultimately, Best in Show. Class winners usually receive a ribbon; Best of Variety or Group, a rosette; Best of Breed, a trophy and Best in Show, a large trophy. Small cash awards are also given to some of the winners.

CHAPTER NINE

Rabbit Facts

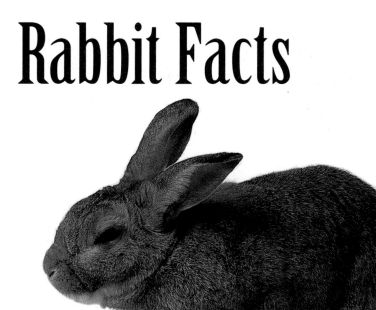

Thousands of years ago, the rabbit was much like the adorable pet of today: Her ears were long, her nose twitched incessantly and she loved to groom her fur to perfection. But in other ways, the rabbit of antiquity and the rabbit of today are worlds apart.

The record of the rabbit's history begins with the earliest known rabbit fossils, which were found in China and Mongolia, and which date back nearly 65 million years to the Paleocene period. In North America, the oldest rabbit fossils are from the Oligocene period 37 million years ago. These ancient species were the evolutionary forebears of today's wild rabbits; modern rabbits differ very little from today's fossil pictures of ancient rabbits.

Africa around 600 B.C., when they were used for their meat and fur. They were traded extensively first by the Phoenicians and then later by other cultures, eventually spreading to America, Australia and New Zealand.

THE RABBIT TODAY

Until the Middle Ages, rabbits were considered a strictly agricultural commodity and were not raised as pets. However, during the fifth century, monasteries in France began keeping rabbits just for the enjoyment of creating different colored coats.

In the 1700s, individuals began keeping rabbits as pets, and in the mid-1800s, rabbit owners who had originally used their animals only for food and fur started to develop specific breeds. Shortly thereafter, these owners began showing their rabbits at competitions. The hobby of showing and breeding rabbits was unregulated until the mid-1930s when the British Rabbit Council was formed. The goal of the council was to govern the fancy by supervising various rabbit clubs and registering rabbits throughout Great Britain.

Rabbits first made the move from wild animals to domestic pets sometime during the late nineteenth century.

RABBITS AND HUMANS

The first signs of mankind's relationship with the rabbit appear in Spanish cave paintings dating from the Stone Age. Artists painted rabbits and hares, along with other animals, on the walls of caves during the Pleistocene period. During this time, the rabbit migrated down to southwestern Europe in an effort to escape the great cold of the Ice Age.

The descendants of the Ice Age rabbits were domesticated near the Mediterranean region in Europe and

The domestic rabbit population in the United States was probably first introduced by early explorers, although there is little written about the animal in America before the late 1800s. Rabbits were used primarily as food here until breeding and showing caught on late in the nineteenth century.

Once showing and breeding became popular activities in the early 1900s, the American Rabbit Breeders Association (ARBA) was founded to promote, encourage and develop the rabbit industry in the United States. ARBA is still the governing body for the rabbit fancy in this country. (See chapter 8 for more on ARBA.)

RABBITS IN POPULAR CULTURE

The rabbit is a favorite subject in contemporary literature, particularly in fiction written for children. *The Tale of Peter Rabbit*, the story of a disobedient young bunny named Peter, has been read and loved by children around the world. The names of the characters in this book by Beatrix Potter have become synonymous with rabbits everywhere: Peter, Flopsy, Mopsy and Cottontail.

Another book about rabbits, *Watership Down*, by Richard Adams, has gained great notoriety, and deservedly so. Using natural rabbit behaviors to create a story about a group of rabbits trying to find a new home in the English countryside, Adams produced one of the

RABBIT LORE

Throughout its history, the rabbit has had a notable affect on humankind. Aside from viewing the rabbit as a source of food and warmth, many cultures have also praised the rabbit for its swiftness and wit.

The most recognizable folktale involving a lagomorph is the story of the tortoise and the hare. Originally a fable from Africa, the story was later adopted and made famous by Aesop. The moral of the fable was designed to show children that, regardless of how confident they are, they should not cut corners in life, as the hare did.

Native American peoples have revered the rabbit throughout history, and some tribes still view it as an important part of their culture. The Algonquins believed that the Great Hare rebuilt the world after an enormous flood, repopulating the world with his offspring. Consequently, according to the story, all humankind is related to the hare.

MORE RABBIT LORE

The Iroquois tribe tells of a time when hunters came upon a large rabbit in a clearing. This rabbit turned out to be the chief of all rabbits. As the hunters stood by and watched, the Rabbit Chief summoned all his fellow rabbits and began a joyous dance. When the hunters returned to their village telling of what they had seen, a wise old woman explained to them that they had been shown a special dance meant to thank the rabbit for the food and warmth that it gave to them in the forms of its flesh and its fur. To this day, the Iroquois people still honor the rabbit with this very dance.

While Europeans believe that they see a man's face when they look up at the moon, some Eastern cultures see a rabbit, and believe this lunar creature to be the ruler of all the rabbits on Earth.

Of course, the Easter Bunny is probably the most famous legendary rabbit in our culture. In the German legend, a bird is turned into a rabbit by the Goddess of Spring. This bird-turned-rabbit continues to lay eggs, however. Thus, the popular Eastertime connection between bunnies and eggs.

most enjoyable animal stories ever written. *Watership Down* not only served to educate the public about rabbit behavior when it was published, but also stirred some sympathy for the plight of the rabbit in today's rapidly developing world.

Literature is not the only realm of popular culture in which rabbits are featured. One of the most famous rabbits of all is Bugs Bunny, the animated creation of Warner Brothers Studios. A staple in children's cartoons since the 1940s, Bugs Bunny continues to be a favorite personality among kids and the adults who grew up with him.

The widespread and widely noted presence of rabbits throughout history and throughout cultures is indicative of the many ways in which these curious and lovable animals enhance the lives of the humans who interact with them. The current increase in the number of households that keep rabbits as pets is the logical next chapter in the history of the rabbit.

CHAPTER TEN

Bunny Breeds

When the rabbit was first domesticated, there was only one "breed." Now, however, there are forty-five breeds of rabbits recognized by the American Rabbit Breeders Association. Obviously, this wide variety means that choosing one particular breed over another can be a daunting task.

CHOOSING A BREED

When determining which breed to acquire, keep your needs and lifestyle in mind. If you live in a small space and don't have room for a large cage, you may want to consider one of the dwarf breeds. If your time is limited, you'll definitely want to stay away from the wooly breeds, as they require frequent grooming. If you have older children who plan to handle and maybe even show their rabbits, you'll want to get a smaller breed that they can easily lift.

COAT VARIETIES

There are four different kinds of fur, or coats, on rabbits.

ANGORA—The long and fluffy Angora coat is often used for spinning because of its warmth. Because it is used to make clothing, the

Angora coat is often referred to as wool. The fur stands away from the rabbit's body, giving it a very fuzzy, hairy appearance.

REX—Rex fur is shorter than standard fur and is cottony and airy to the touch. It is much thicker than standard fur, and stands upright instead of laying flat against the rabbit's body. Rex fur also has a double coat.

SATIN—Satin fur has fine, somewhat translucent hairshafts that make it look silky and shiny. Satin coats are about the same length as standard fur coats, but are distinguishable by their luster.

STANDARD—Standard rabbit fur is the coat that most people imagine when they think about rabbits. It comes in two layers, an overcoat and undercoat. Both layers are approximately 1 inch in length. The undercoat is soft and insulates the rabbit against cold temperatures.

COAT COLOR PATTERNS

As a whole, rabbit coats display an astounding number of colors and patterns, each with its own unique beauty. To make identification easier, these colors have been assigned to specific groups. A general definition of each group follows.

AGOUTI PATTERN—The hairshaft on an agouti-colored rabbit has three or more bands of color, usually with a dark-gray base. This is the color pattern seen in wild rabbits. Agouti-colored rabbits come in chestnut, chocolate, sable, lilac and smoke pearl.

BRINDLE PATTERN—Brindle is an intermingling of two colors, one dark and one light. The brindle pattern appears consistently throughout the body.

BROKEN PATTERN—There are two different subdivisions within the broken pattern: bicolor and tricolor. A bicolored broken pattern consists of any standard rabbit color in combination with white. A tricolored rabbit, on the other hand, will have two other colors in addition to white.

MARKED PATTERN—Marked pattern rabbits are usually white, and have one other color that appears in a distinct pattern over the entire body.

POINTED WHITE PATTERN— This type of rabbit is all white with a darker color on its nose, ears, feet and tail. These markings are much like those of a Siamese cat.

SELF PATTERN—Rabbits whose coats consist of only one color solidly covering their entire bodies are said to carry a self pattern.

SHADED PATTERN—This pattern looks much like it sounds. Shaded rabbits show a gradual shift in color, beginning with a darker color on their backs, heads, necks, ears, legs and tails.

SOLID PATTERN—This pattern is similar to the self pattern, except that it may include agouti and other mixed-color fur, as long as the colors do not create a pattern or a distinct marking.

TICKED PATTERN—This consists of a base color throughout the majority of the rabbit's fur, with the addition of contrasting solid or tipped guard hairs.

Rabbits, like this 9-day-old bunny, are born in a variety of colors and coat patterns.

WIDE BAND PATTERN—Rabbits of this coloration have the same color on their bodies, heads, ears, tails and feet. Their eye circles, the underside of their tails, their jaws and their stomachs have a lighter coloration.

RABBIT COLORS

Each breed has its own breed standard and selection of color varieties.

BEIGE—Rabbits of this color have the pigment all over their bodies except on the napes of their necks, which are lighter.

BLUE—The blue coloration can be described as a medium shade of gray with a blue or lavender cast.

CASTOR—A rich, dark chestnut color, castor is sometimes also described as mahogany brown.

CHINCHILLA—The standard chinchilla coloration consists of a blend of black and pearl with a dark-gray base.

CHOCOLATE—A deep, dark brown, this coloration features a light-gray undercoat.

FAWN—Fawn-colored rabbits have a deep golden color over their backs, flanks and chests.

LILAC—This coloration consists of a medium-gray hue with a pinkish tint that is present over the rabbit's entire body.

LYNX—The body and the top of a lynx-colored rabbit's tail are tinged with lilac and light orange, and a sharper orange color shows through from underneath. There are white areas underneath the tail, belly and jaw.

OPAL—The hairshaft of an opal-colored rabbit features a pale bluish color on top with a fawn band below it.

SIAMESE—Siamese-colored rabbits look a lot like Siamese cats. They have dark-brown color on their ears, head, feet, belly and tail, with a

Blue Torte
Dutch Rabbit.

lighter body color distinct from the point colors. The eyes are brown.

SQUIRREL—The hairshaft on a rabbit with the squirrel coloration consists of a blend of gray and white bands. The color extends from the rabbit's back down along its sides, where it is met by white on the belly and on top of the hind feet.

STEEL—This color configuration comes in black, blue, chocolate and lilac, as well as sable and smoke pearl colors. The entire body of the rabbit is covered with one of the above colors, the hairs of which are diffused with a small amount of gold or silver tipping, depending on whether the rabbit is a gold steel or a silver steel.

TAN PATTERN—This coloration features a solid color on the head, back, sides, outside of the ears, back legs, front of the forelegs and top of the tail.

TORTOISESHELL—Rabbits with this coloration sport a lively orange on their bodies, which mingles into a grayish-blue shadowing over the rump and haunches.

81

POPULAR BREEDS

Fuzzy Lop Rabbit.

AMERICAN—The American rabbit, which has been in existence for nearly 100 years, comes in two color varieties: blue and white. The blue variety has blue-gray eyes, while the white version has pink eyes. Compact in appearance, the American is a medium-size rabbit weighing around 10 pounds.

AMERICAN FUZZY LOP—The Fuzzy Lop, originally created by

Dutch Rabbit.

Angoras come in an astounding array of beautiful colors. Because of the Angora's dense coat, which grows to about 3 inches in length, the breed requires a good deal of grooming.

BELGIAN HARE—Despite its name, the Belgian Hare is actually a domestic rabbit, not a hare. However, its long legs and ears do give it the appearance of a hare, hence its name.

BEVEREN—Not as frequently seen in the United States as some other breeds, the Beveren was developed in Europe and is colored either white, blue or black. A large rabbit weighing about 10 pounds, the Beveren has a thick, silky coat.

crossbreeding the Holland Lop and the Angora, is found in a wide variety of colors.

AMERICAN SABLE—This rabbit is well-named, because its coat, the result of several crosses with the chinchilla rabbit, is a beautiful dark brown.

ANGORA—There are four types of Angora rabbits: English Angora, French Angora, Satin Angora and Giant Angora. Each one is a separate breed and has the long, wooly hair typical of the Angora family.

BRITANNIA PETITE—The tiny Britannia Petite is an all-white or black otter–colored rabbit that weighs only about 2 pounds.

CALIFORNIAN—This very popular rabbit looks very much like a Siamese cat, with its white coat and black-tipped ears, nose, feet and tail. Somewhat large in size, the typical Californian weighs about 9 pounds.

CHAMPAGNE D'ARGENT—The coat of this rabbit contains a marvelous mixture of colored hairs, resulting in a wonderful silver-looking effect.

CHECKERED GIANT—The Checkered Giant is available in black and blue color varieties. The breed is typically white with dark markings, including a "butterfly" on the nose, dark ears, dark circles around the eyes, spots on the cheeks and various other dark patches on the body.

CHINCHILLA—There are three types of Chinchilla rabbit: Standard, American and Giant. All three types have the coloring of an actual chinchilla and are popular pets because of their attractive coats.

CINNAMON—This breed is available only in the reddish color indicative of its name. The ears, face and feet bear a darker shade of this same color. Occasional shades of gray on various parts of its body contribute to this breed's unusual appearance.

CREME D'ARGENT—The Creme D'Argent, which originated in

France, is a handsome rabbit with an exquisitely colored coat of pale orange.

DUTCH—The Dutch is an extremely popular rabbit, and is easily recognizable because of its markings. Available in six color varieties, the Dutch has a dark head with a white nose and blaze, and dark "britches."

DWARF HOTOT—Found only in white with dark eyes, the Dwarf Hotot weighs about 3 pounds and was bred down from the Hotot in the 1970s.

ENGLISH SPOT—The English Spot, or English for short, is reminiscent of a Dalmatian with its white coat and dark spots. A capped nose, dark ears, eye rings and a stripe along the back are all characteristic of this breed, which weighs about 8 pounds.

FLEMISH GIANT—Massive in size, the Flemish Giant is the largest breed of rabbit and weighs more than 14 pounds. Found in steel gray, light gray, black, blue, white, sandy and fawn, this breed is very popular as a pet despite its large size.

83

BREEDS RECOGNIZED BY THE AMERICAN RABBIT BREEDERS ASSOCIATION

American	Harlequin
American Fuzzy Lop	Havana
American Sable	Himalayan
Angora, English	Hotot
Angora, French	Jersey Wooly
Angora, Giant	Lilac
Angora, Satin	Lop, English
Belgian Hare	Lop, French
Beveren	Lop, Holland
Californian	Lop, Mini
Champagne D'Argent	Mini Rex
Checkered Giant	Netherland Dwarf
Chinchilla, American	New Zealand
Chinchilla, Giant	Palomino
Chinchilla, Standard	Polish
Cinnamon	Rex
Creme D'Argent	Rhinelander
Dutch	Satin
Dwarf Hotot	Silver
English Spot	Silver Fox
Flemish Giant	Silver Marten
Florida White	Tan

FLORIDA WHITE—The Florida White, as its name implies, comes in white only and has pink eyes. It weighs about 5 pounds.

HARLEQUIN—The Harlequin, an interesting, medium-size and unusually marked rabbit of about 8 pounds, was developed in France in the 1800s. The heads of Harlequin rabbits are divided in half by color; each rabbit can look like two different animals when viewed from one side and then the other! Harlequin base colors are black, blue, lilac and chocolate.

HAVANA—While it first appeared in chocolate, the Havana is now available in blue and black varieties as well. Prized for its coat, the Havana is short and compact, weighing about 6 pounds.

HIMALAYAN—The Himalayan breed has existed for many years, reportedly originating near the Himalayan Mountains. Distinctive because of its white coat and blue or black markings, this rabbit is small in size and usually weighs only 4 pounds.

HOTOT—In France, this breed is known as the Blanc de Hotot, or the "white of Hotot," Hotot being the area where it was developed. Available only in a frosty white color with thin black eye circles, the Hotot is a medium-size rabbit weighing around 9 pounds.

JERSEY WOOLY—A recently developed breed of rabbit created in the 1970s through crossbreeding, the Jersey Wooly was produced specifically for its luxurious coat. The fur of the Jersey Wooly is available in the agouti, pointed white, self, shaded and tan pattern color groups. A small rabbit, the Jersey Wooly weighs about 3 pounds.

LILAC—The Lilac comes in one color, a light pinkish gray. Weighing about 7 pounds, the body of the Lilac is substantial and compact.

LOP—The Lop rabbits are probably the most distinctive and easily recognizable of all the breeds. Lop breeds of the past included rabbits whose ears flopped forward over their faces and rabbits whose ears both flopped over to the same side.

These breeds are extinct now, and the Lop we see today is the Lop of choice.

The modern Lop has huge ears, which flop down beside its head like a Basset Hound's, and give it the special look unique to the breed.

There are four breeds of Lop rabbits: the English Lop, French Lop, Holland Lop and Mini Lop. Each breed is unique in both its appearance and history.

The English Lop is one of the oldest breeds of domestic rabbit still in existence. Developed at least as early as the 1800s, the English Lop was the first of the lop-eared breeds.

85

Lop Rabbits.

The French Lop was first developed in France in the 1800s out of a breeding between the English Lop and the Flemish Giant. The French Lop differs from the English in that it is characterized by a heavier stature and shorter ears.

The Holland Lop, a dwarf breed of Lop, was created in Holland in the 1960s. It displays the same color varieties as the French and English: agouti, broken, pointed white, self, solid, shaded and ticked.

The Mini Lop is also a relatively new breed of Lop. The Mini Lop is similar to the French Lop, but its mere 5-pound weight makes it significantly smaller.

MINI REX—The Mini Rex was developed using the standard-size Rex. Weighing about 4 pounds, this breed is available in the same color varieties and colors as its larger cousin, the Rex.

NETHERLAND DWARF—The very popular Netherland Dwarf is the smallest of all domestic rabbits, weighing no more than 2 pounds. Its tiny stature, wide range of colors, small ears and large eyes make it a very popular pet.

NEW ZEALAND—The New Zealand is available in three distinct color varieties: white, black and red. Typical New Zealand rabbits weigh about 10 pounds.

PALOMINO—A relatively new breed, the Palomino was developed in the United States and comes in two color varieties: golden and lynx. Weighing about 9 pounds, the Palomino has a slightly arched back.

POLISH—A tiny rabbit weighing only about 3 pounds, the Polish is believed to have developed in England in the 1800s. Some experts believe that the name does not refer to the country of Poland, but rather to its shiny coat.

REX—The fur of the Rex rabbit looks and feels like plush velvet. This breed, which comes in a wide variety of colors, is very popular as a pet and show rabbit.

RHINELANDER—The Rhinelander has an unusual coloration that can best be described as patches of calico, much like those that appear on a calico cat. The breed's base color is white, and its nose, ears, cheeks, eyes, back and

Seal Rex Rabbit.

sides are marked with black and orange.

SATIN—The Satin is so named because of its soft, shiny coat. The Satin is a medium-size rabbit that weighs about 9 pounds.

SILVER—The Silver got its name from its coat's unique coloring, a silvery sheen created by a mixture of white hairs against a dark background. Available in black, brown and fawn, Silver rabbits weigh between 4 and 7 pounds.

SILVER FOX—Originally bred in Europe for its fur, the Silver Fox has an unusual coat. Measuring 1 inch or more in length with a thick undercoat, the fur of the Silver Fox comes in black or blue varieties.

SILVER MARTEN—Created using the Chinchilla rabbit, the Silver Marten has guard hairs that are gray-tipped on a dark background of black, blue, chocolate or sable.

TAN—The color and markings of the Tan are reminiscent of a Doberman Pinscher, particularly the black and chocolate varieties. The top part of the body is dark, while the underside is tan. The tan coloring also appears around the eyes and nose, under the neck and inside the rims of the ears.

CHAPTER ELEVEN

Recommended Reading

BOOKS

Bennet, Bob. *Rabbits as a Hobby.* Neptune, NJ: TFH, 1991.

Campbell, Darlene. *Proper Care of Rabbits.* Neptune, NJ: TFH, 1992.

Fraser, Samantha. *Hop to It!: A Guide to Training Your Pet Rabbit.* Hauppauge, NY: Barron's Educational Series, Inc., 1991.

Mays, Marianne. *Pet Owner's Guide to Rabbits.* New York: Howell Book House, 1995.

Robinson, David. *Encyclopedia of Pet Rabbits.* Neptune, NJ: TFH, 1979.

Vriends-Parent, Lucia. *The New Rabbit Handbook.* Hauppauge, NY: Barron's Educational Series, Inc., 1989.

Wegler, Monika. *Rabbits: A Complete Pet Owner's Manual.* Hauppauge, NY: Barron's Educational Series, Inc., 1990.

MAGAZINES

House Rabbit Journal
House Rabbit Society
1524 Benton St.
Alameda, CA 94501
A publication that provides information on how to live with indoor rabbits.

Rabbits Only
P.O. Box 207
Holbrook, NY 11741
A publication for rabbit fanciers.

Rabbits USA
P.O. Box 6050
Mission Viejo, CA 92690
(714) 855-8822
An annual magazine for rabbit owners.

CHAPTER TWELVE

Resources

NATIONAL ASSOCIATIONS

AMERICAN RABBIT BREEDERS ASSOCIATION (ARBA)
1925 S. Main St.
Box 426
Bloomington, IL 61702
(309) 664-7500
Official governing body for rabbit shows in the United States. Contact
ARBA for information on affiliated breed clubs.

HOUSE RABBIT SOCIETY
P.O. Box 1201
Alameda, CA 94501
(510) 521-4631
Membership includes a subscription to the *House Rabbit Journal*, which contains information on how to live with indoor rabbits. Send a self-addressed, stamped envelope to the above address for more information.

NATIONAL 4-H COUNCIL
7100 Connecticut Ave.
Chevy Chase, MD 20815
(301) 961-2800
Can provide general information on 4-H.